A TEEN MANIA DEVOTIONAL

Regal

From Gospel Light
Ventura, California, U.S.A.

Published by Regal
From Gospel Light
Ventura, California, U.S.A.
www.regalbooks.com
Printed in the U.S.A.

All dictionary definitions are from *Webster's New Collegiate Dictionary*, 10th edition.

Library of Congress Cataloging-in-Publication Data
Luce, Ron.
Connecting with God : a teen mania devotional / Ron Luce.
p. cm.
ISBN 978-0-8307-4716-0 (trade paper)
1. Christian teenagers—Prayers and devotions. I. Title.
BV4850.L845 2009
242'.63—dc22
2008044819

1 2 3 4 5 6 7 8 9 10 11 12 13 14 15 / 15 14 13 12 11 10 09

Rights for publishing this book outside the U.S.A. or in non-English languages are administered by Gospel Light Worldwide, an international not-for-profit ministry. For additional information, please visit www.glww.org, email info@glww.org, or write to Gospel Light Worldwide, 1957 Eastman Avenue, Ventura, CA 93003, U.S.A.

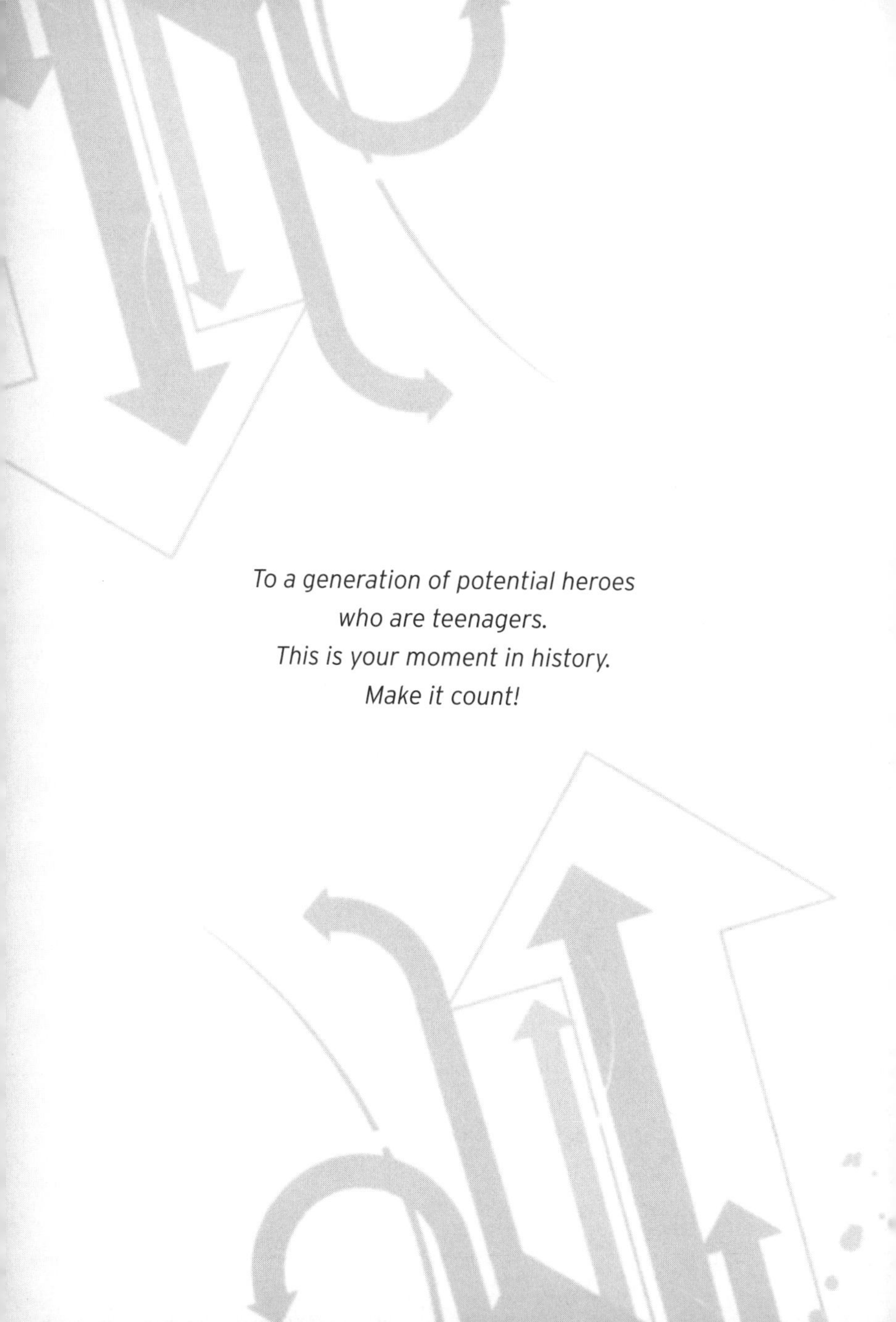

To a generation of potential heroes
who are teenagers.
This is your moment in history.
Make it count!

CONTENTS

Introduction 5

Week 1: A Call to Arms 7
Week 2: Having a Quiet Time 21
Week 3: It's All About Love 35
Week 4: Transform Your Mind, Transform Your Life 47
Week 5: Studying the Bible 63
Week 6: Accountability Friendships 79
Week 7: Living a Lifestyle of Holiness 95
Week 8: Courtship Over Dating 109
Week 9: Honoring Your Parents 127
Week 10: Commit to Your Youth Group and Church 143
Week 11: Be the One to Start a Revolution 161
Week 12: The Adventure of a Lifetime 179
Week 13: Blasting into the Rest of Your Life 195

Appendix A: Record of Scriptures Memorized 208
Appendix B: Record of Continuing Commitments 217

INTRODUCTION

This is not a typical book. It's a thirteen-week devotional you can work through by yourself or with a group, but it's *more* than that. It is not supposed to be just one more thing that you read through and then forget what you read. It is designed to get you into action, to push you over the edge to make a big difference in the world.

It is going to be important for you to decide beforehand that you are going to make it all the way through this devotional. The next thirteen weeks could be the turning point that you have been looking for in your life.

I want to encourage you right now to do the following:

1. Make a commitment to have your quiet time every day for the next thirteen weeks.

2. Make a commitment to do everything that you are asked to do (including filling in all the blanks and memorizing all the Scriptures). In the back of the book, there's a place to record each Scripture that you memorize. Make sure you do that each time you've completely memorized a Scripture and you'll be amazed at how much of God's Word you'll be putting in your heart.

3. Find an accountability friend to go through it with you every day. (Choose someone you feel comfortable with. You need to get in each other's face to keep pressing on every day. The big thing here is to make sure that both of you are doing the stuff every day that you are supposed to do.)

Some things in this book will really stretch you out of your comfort zone. Some things will cause you to draw attention to yourself. As a follower of Christ, you have to get people's attention so that they know you are a Christian and that you are not ashamed of the gospel of Jesus Christ. While I do want you to go forth boldly in every area of your life—home, school, work, sports—I would never encourage you to break any laws or rules set forth by your authorities. You want to avoid offending people so much that you actually drive them away from God rather than drive them into His presence. Keeping this in mind, get ready to step out of your comfort zone and into the wild, exciting life of a follower of Christ!

I commit to go all the way through this devotional.
I will start on ______________________ *and*
plan to finish on _________________________.

____

Follower of Christ's Signature

____

Accountability Partner's Signature

____

Youth Pastor's or Parent's Signature

WEEK 1

A CALL TO ARMS

TO FOLLOW CHRIST

Follow Me, and I will make you fishers of men.

Matthew 4:19

God is raising up a fresh, fiery brand of young passionate Christians who want to change the world. The purpose of this book is to show you how to become one of them—a true follower of Christ. It is time to wake up. Check out what God is doing, and jump into the middle of it!

Followers of Christ take Jesus at His word. They actually believe it is possible to live out what He teaches. They have quit just listening to sermons, and decided to live them. They have decided to go after God with everything in them.

Young followers of Christ are determined to make their lives count. They are frustrated by sermons about how God is going to "use young people." They already *do all they can to BE* the young people God is using *NOW*. They are not satisfied with an average, pretty-good Christian life where people think they are saints if they stay off drugs. They have something so big in their hearts that they have to do something with it or it will eat them alive.

These young firebrands have quit looking to the world. They are looking to God for their marching orders. True followers find their purpose in Him and in doing what pleases Him.

Think about what kind of a follower of Christ you want to be, and take a few minutes to pray about it. Write out your thoughts.

____

____

____

____

____

____

SEEK GOD FIRST

Seek first the kingdom of God and His righteousness, and all these things shall be added to you.

Matthew 6:33

In a very real way, followers of Christ have checked out of this world's system because they value different things. Their hearts don't belong to things; they belong to God. True followers don't ask what God can do for them; instead, they ask what they can do for God. They are not caught up with clothes, clichés, cars and cool things; they are excited about seeking, loving, serving and knowing God.

Christianity is not a part-time thing for followers of Christ. They don't go to church because somebody makes them go. They want to go, and can't wait to dive back into more of God! They have found their identity in Him and in His plan for their lives. They have found the reason they were created, and nothing will stop them.

Followers of Christ know that they are here to change this world with the love of Christ. They are here to make this world a different place. They want less sin in the world when they are finished with it. They want fewer broken hearts when they are gone. They want to see more people going to heaven when they are finished pouring their lives out for this world.

They have found something that demands their all, and they don't mind giving it for Him. They have found something worth sinking their teeth into, and they are not about to let go! They have made a discovery so important that it has altered the rest of their lives.

You can have all the money, fame, prestige and toys this world has to offer, but until you have changed the world, you have not accomplished anything. What do you want to accomplish?

Take four minutes to memorize Matthew 6:33. Write out what it means to you.

Now go to appendix A and write out Matthew 6:33, recording that you memorized this verse.

TO BE BORN AGAIN

I tell you the truth, no one can see the kingdom of God unless he is born again.

John 3:3, *NIV*

Jesus told Nicodemus that there is only one way into heaven, and that way is to be born again. Like any of us might do, he asked a simple question: How can somebody enter his mother's womb and be born all over again (see v. 4)? Jesus explained the answer very clearly and simply: "No one can enter the kingdom of God unless he is born of water and the Spirit" (v. 5). You must be born physically—"of water"—to be eligible to go to heaven, but you also have to be born spiritually.

If you're alive on the earth, then you have met the first qualification: You were born physically. However, that is not enough. You must be born spiritually as well.

Jesus went on to say, "Flesh gives birth to flesh, but the Spirit gives birth to spirit" (v. 6). He was talking about being born of the Spirit. The Holy Spirit gives birth to spirit. Verse 8 says, "The wind blows wherever it pleases. You hear its sound, but you cannot tell where it comes from or where it is going." Although you cannot see the wind, you can hear it and see its effects because you see the leaves blowing in the trees.

It's the same way when the Holy Spirit comes into your life. You can't see the Spirit, but you can see His effect on your life. He changes your life, and you become a brand-new person.

When you give your life to Jesus, you really come alive on the inside. Your spirit is made brand-new, and you're born again. When you make a radical commitment to give your life to Jesus, you believe that He died on the cross for you and rose from the dead. You say, "Now I am going to live for You." A transformation happens inside like you were never alive before. Basically, He is saying,

"There is only one way to get into the kingdom of heaven. You have to be born into it."

Think of a barking dog. You don't get mad at the dog just because he barks. He was born a barker, and he has to bark because that is the only kind of noise he can make. No matter how much you try to get him to stop, he is going to bark because he was born a dog.

It works the same way for people. Everyone is born in sin as a sinner. No matter how much anyone tries, everyone still does wrong things because everyone is born in sin. The only way to become a person in the kingdom of God is to be born into the kingdom of God. You must be made a brand-new person. That is exactly what happens when you give your life to Jesus. You sell out everything to Him. He makes you a brand-new person. That is what Jesus tried to explain to Nicodemus.

If you have given your life to Jesus, then it is time to rejoice. You didn't pray some cheese-ball prayer. God completely changed you inside and made you a brand-new person. Take a few minutes right now and thank God for making you a brand-new person. Think about John 3:3 today. Keep repeating it and chewing on it throughout the day.

If you have never prayed to give your life to the Lord, then pray this prayer from your heart and start your brand-new life today:

> *Dear Lord Jesus, I commit with all my heart to give You my life. I believe that You died on the cross for me and that You rose from the dead. From now on, I'm going to call You my Lord, my Boss. From now on, I will live my life for You. You're the center of my life. Forgive me, Lord. Clean out my heart. Clean out my life, and I will live for You every day for the rest of my life. In Jesus' name, amen.*

DAY 4

YOUR RELATIONSHIP WITH JESUS (PART 1)

But as many as received Him, to them He gave the right to become children of God, to those who believe in His name.

John 1:12

What is a relationship with Jesus?

The Bible says that if you have given your life to Jesus, if you have been born again, you have become a child of God. You have become a son or daughter of the Most High God. Unlike your physical birth, this did not happen because of some human decision; it happened because spiritually you became a brand-new person. You got plugged in to God spiritually. You became connected to Him.

So, you have a relationship with God through His Son, Jesus Christ. You are just like a child of a father. You are His offspring, and He now calls you a son or a daughter. Now He wants to help you grow, to be strong, to become a mature and responsible human being. Just like a father would provide for his daughter or his son, He will provide food, clothes and a roof over your head.

God wants to take care of you, nurture you and help you grow up to be sound, stable and courageous.

God doesn't want you to pray a little prayer and go on with your life in the same direction. When you pray to give your life to Him, He wants to perform a radical, drastic transformation so that you become just like a little child—a baby in Christ—and He wants to feed you, care for you and watch you grow.

You may or may not have a loving and involved earthly father in your life, but your heavenly Father is the best father anyone could ever have. Psalm 68:5 says that God is "a father to the fatherless." Ask Him to be your Father right now and to show you the kind of love a true father has for his children.

YOUR RELATIONSHIP WITH JESUS (PART 2)

But as many as received Him, to them He gave the right to become children of God, to those who believe in His name.

John 1:12

God feeds you with His Word. He feeds you by teaching you and filling your life with wisdom from the Bible. He helps you grow and become mature in areas of your life that are not all together, areas in which you have experienced some problems or have some bad habits. God is not mad at you. He understands that you were born with a sinful nature, but now He has given you a new heart, and He wants you to grow up in these areas.

List three areas that you feel you need to grow up in.

The kind of relationship God wants to have with you is one that puts your life back together. Maybe the world has really stomped on you and ripped your life apart in one way or another. God specializes in putting broken lives back together.

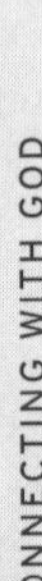

List two or three areas of your life that you feel have been ripped apart and that you need God's help to put back together.

Please understand from the very beginning that the Bible says that God loves you like a son or a daughter and He is out for your best. He wants to take the areas you have listed—and even other areas that you don't know about yet—and help you grow and become mature. Pray about these areas right now:

> *Father, I thank You that You know everything about my life—my past, my present and my future. Lord, I commit these areas to You and ask You to help me grow to become a strong and mature man [or woman] of God in these areas. Put my life back together just as a loving earthly father would help his son [or daughter] do. Help me get to be what You want me to be. In Jesus' name, amen.*

DAY 6

KEEPING YOUR RELATIONSHIP WITH JESUS ALIVE

This is love: not that we loved God, but that he loved us and sent his Son as an atoning sacrifice for our sins.

1 John 4:10, *NIV*

Keeping your relationship with Jesus alive is about loving Him with everything in you. It is not about doing things to see how good you can be. It is about loving Him with every action you take. It is not about playing the "church game" or seeing how spiritual you can look. It is about loving God with your whole being, the very core of who you are.

The relationship God wants with you is one in which you love Him with everything you are because you know He loves you with everything He is.

The Bible says, "God is love" (1 John 4:8). Anytime you get close to God, you're getting close to love. It's what He is made of. He wants a relationship in which you love Him willingly and are able to receive His love.

A lot of people think that having a relationship with God is just about following a bunch of rules and regulations and being good so that God will love you more. It has nothing to do with that. It has nothing to do with whether you keep the rules or not. He loved you before you ever gave your heart to Him. When you begin to understand His love, you *want* to love Him back.

God's love is about having a real relationship—a friendship—with Him, and becoming the person you have always wanted to be and He wants you to be. Because you have fallen in love with the most incredible God of all humankind and realize that He is real, you want to follow Him with all your heart.

No one in the world loves us enough to die for us, especially if they knew all of our worst secrets. But that's what God did for each of us. Think about this: God loved you first, even before you loved Him.

Take a few minutes to meditate on what Jesus did for you, and then write down your thoughts.

DAY 7

COMMIT TO BE A TRUE FOLLOWER OF CHRIST

This is love for God: to obey his commands. And his commands are not burdensome, for everyone born of God overcomes the world.

1 John 5:3-4

Some people say that they love God, but they do things that are totally against God. They don't really know what they are saying when they talk about love. This is made evident in the way they throw the word "love" around so half-heartedly. They say that they love peanut butter and jelly, pizza, and, oh yeah, God, too.

Love of God is a different kind of love. It is about loving Him so much that you commit everything to Him. Think about what it would be like for a girl to hear a guy say to her, "I love you, and I really want to marry you." A year later he says, "I love you, and I really, really want to marry you." Five years later he says, "Honey, I love you, and I really, really want to marry you." Ten years later he says, "Honey, I love you so much, and I really, really want to marry you."

After a while, the girl starts thinking, *Wait a minute! If you do love me, then do something about it. If you really love me, then commit.* That is what loving God is about. It is about loving Him so much that you commit and lock in. When you choose to marry somebody, you're not forced to do it. You want to marry that person because you love the person so much that you want to commit.

That is the same kind of relationship that God wants—that you love Him so much that you commit your life to Him. By your commitment, you agree to live by the principles and the guidelines of the rules that He puts in the Scriptures. Are you willing to make this commitment now?

I commit to be a true follower of Christ. I will seek God, love God and serve God with everything I have. I understand that I have been born again, and I want my Father's help to mature in my faith. I want to keep my relationship with Jesus alive. I commit my life to God.

______________________________ Your Signature

______________ Date

WEEK 2

HAVING A QUIET TIME

DAY 1

WHAT IS A QUIET TIME? (PART 1)

I am the good shepherd; and I know My sheep, and am known by My own.

John 10:14

In this passage, Jesus describes the kind of relationship He wants with you. He compares it to the relationship between a shepherd and his sheep. A shepherd and his sheep have a very intimate relationship. Maybe you have this relationship with your pet dog or cat—it knows your voice when you call its name. In the same way, a shepherd's voice is very distinct to his sheep.

A shepherd walks and hangs out with his sheep. He takes them to different mountains where he knows there is good grass for them, and he really watches over them. Jesus said He wants the same kind of relationship with you:

> I am the good shepherd. The good shepherd gives His life for the sheep. But he who is a hireling and not the shepherd, one who does not own the sheep, sees the wolf coming and leaves the sheep and flees; and the wolf catches the sheep and scatters them. The hireling flees because he is a hireling and does not care about the sheep. I am the good shepherd; and I know My sheep, and am known by My own. As the Father knows Me, even so I know the Father; and I lay down My life for the sheep. And other sheep I have which are not of this fold; them also I must bring, and they will hear My voice; and there will be one flock and one shepherd (John 10:11-16).

Jesus wants you to hang out with Him long enough to learn His voice. He doesn't want you to be a stranger He sees only twice a year at Christmas and Easter. He wants to see you often. He wants you hanging out with Him so much that you are listening to the things that He has to say.

A quiet time is a time for you to do just that. You get into the Bible, pray and listen. You pray about the things He puts on your heart, and He speaks back to you. You start your whole day by getting tight with Him.

You've got to be committed to having quiet times and to keeping quiet times, no matter what. It doesn't matter how busy you are. It doesn't matter what happens to your schedule.

You are compelled to say, "I have to get up. I have to pray because I have to get fed. I have to get close to my Shepherd, and I don't care what other people do. If I don't get fed from Him today, I will die."

Memorize John 10:14 and chew on it all day. Remind yourself that Jesus is the Shepherd and you are His sheep. He knows you, and you know Him.

How do you feel about knowing that Jesus is your Shepherd? Write down your thoughts.

____

____

____

____

____

____

____

____

WHAT IS A QUIET TIME? (PART 2)

I am the good shepherd; and I know My sheep, and am known by My own.

John 10:14

A quiet time is an intimate, face-to-face, heart-to-heart connection with God through His Son, Jesus Christ. It's the time when you actually build your relationship with Jesus. Specifically, it is a time for you to get up every day and read the Bible and pray and get closer to Him.

A lot of people think, *I prayed a prayer, but I don't feel closer to God*; or *I felt really close to God when I was at the Acquire the Fire convention* [or some other retreat or camp], *but now I don't feel very close to Him.* You're not going to feel close to anybody if you're not spending time with that person.

A quiet time is an expression of your commitment to be a true follower of Christ. It's as if you're saying, "Lord, I'm going to make sure that I don't accidentally get farther and farther away from You. In fact, I'm going to use this time to get closer and closer to You. I'm going to use it as a time to get fed by You and to get filled up with You and to understand more of You." Before you do anything else, start your day with God. Talk to Him, seek Him in His Word and pray through your day. Make it your top priority.

Maybe you've never had a quiet time with God before. Start thinking about what kind of quiet time you want to have and where you want to have it. Think about what time you need to get up in order to have enough time to read your Bible and pray before you start your day with the world.

What time will that be?

DAY 3

WHAT TO DO DURING QUIET TIMES

Grow in the grace and knowledge of our Lord and Savior Jesus Christ.

2 Peter 3:18

"All right. I get up to have this quiet-time thing at 6:30 in the morning. I'm up earlier than I'm supposed to be. I'm a little bit tired. What am I supposed to do during this quiet time anyway?"

Great question! Your quiet time should be the most revolutionary time of your day. It should be the most exciting part of your day. This is more important than meeting with the president of the United States. This is meeting with the God of the universe, the God who made everything. He wants to meet with you to make your heart more like His, to make your life more like His. He wants to do surgery on you and allow you to hear more of His voice, to understand more of who He is and what He is about. It is an appointment with God—something that you don't want to miss.

You can do a lot of things during this time. Make it different every day. In Psalm 119, David described several ways to spend time with God. Here are some things you can do:

- Get into the Word. Begin to read through the Bible. Psalm 119:11 says, "Your word I have hidden in my heart, that I might not sin against You." You need to hide the Word in your heart so that you will not sin.
- Quote the Scripture. Psalm 119:13 says, "With my lips I have declared all the judgments of Your mouth." Talk about the stuff that God is doing. Repeat a Scripture over and over again until you have memorized it.
- Meditate on the Word. Psalm 119:15 says, "I will meditate on Your precepts, and contemplate Your ways." Meditating

is different from memorizing. Meditating on the Word means you just continue to chew on it and chew on it and think about what each word means. Then it begins to come alive to you.

- Give God thanks. Psalm 119:62 says, "At midnight I will rise to give thanks to You, because of Your righteous judgments." During your quiet time, you need to thank God for His Word and who He is. You need to really worship and praise Him. Sometimes this means waking up in the middle of the night to spend time with Him.

- Live the Word. Make a decision to live out the part of the Word that you read during your quiet time. Psalm 119:112 says, "I have inclined my heart to perform Your statutes forever, to the very end." In other words, you make a decision that you are going to go for it. You are going to do what you read in the morning. Even if you don't do anything else, you are at least going to do what you have read this morning.

List some other things you can do during your quiet time with God. How about checking out a Bible study guide? How about keeping a journal of your times together with God? Take the rest of your time this morning and read through a portion of Scripture that you choose. Commit to think about it. Chew on it and live it out today with all your heart.

____

____

____

____

____

____

____

JESUS' QUIET TIME HABIT (PART 1)

Jesus would often go to some place where he could be alone and pray.

Luke 5:16, *CEV*

Luke 5:16 is a picture of Jesus' lifestyle of having quiet times. He had an active relationship with His Father, and He had to be plugged in to God every single day. It didn't matter how late He had stayed up the night before. It didn't matter what it cost. He got up early and found a way to spend time with His Father.

Sometimes we say, "Oh, well, I can still pray with other people around," or "I don't really need to do it every day." But the Bible says that even Jesus got up every day and went away by Himself. He demanded of Himself that He get up to get away from everybody and get tight with His Father.

You may want to live for Jesus and do great things for Him, but the most important thing is what happens in your heart and in your life when no one else is looking. That is what's going to make you the man or woman of God you need to be—full of fire, full of power and full of conviction to live your life for Him every single day.

No one can change the world unless God has changed more of him or her. That is what a quiet time is about. Get up early just like Jesus did, and get tight with God so that you can understand what part of the world He wants you to change each day.

If you are not full of God—if your heart is not full of life—then you have nothing to give this world. Sure, you could use some chewed-up Scripture that you used the day before, or you could use some regurgitated sermon you heard someone preach—but God wants to give you something fresh for today.

To get that new life in you, you need to take on the same habits that Jesus had. Jesus spent a lot of time in prayer. He got up even before the sun rose. In fact, sometimes the disciples got up and started looking for Him, wondering, "Where is Jesus? Where did He go? We can't find Him. We figured that He was so tired from the all the work that He did yesterday that He'd still be asleep."

But Jesus wasn't asleep. He was already up, meeting with God. He knew that if He didn't spend time with God, He wouldn't get filled up. Then He wouldn't have anything to give the world that day. So establishing a quiet time is establishing a lifestyle and a pattern just like Jesus had. He did it every day, and you can do it every day, too.

Take some time and get in the Word. Pray and get full of life right now. People need to hear something from you today that you heard from God. They are going to get it only if you get connected with God before your day begins.

Have your quiet time, and then write down what you heard from God.

JESUS' QUIET TIME HABIT (PART 2)

Jesus would often go to some place where he could be alone and pray.

Luke 5:16, *CEV*

You read this Scripture yesterday. Now take four minutes and repeat this verse over and over again until you have memorized it.

This verse looks at Jesus' lifestyle of having a quiet time. This was not something He thought about casually, that now and then He might pray a little bit. This was an absolute lifestyle. There was no way He could live without it. He demanded of Himself that He get up.

The Bible says that He would often get away to pray. The disciples could not count the number of times. It was not something He did once in a while; it was something that happened so often that they depended on it.

He went to places where He could be alone. Our lives are so busy and so full of activities that we spend very little time alone. We are with a lot of other people or with our video and computer games, media and high-tech stuff; and our minds are busy, busy, busy.

The devil uses all these things—music, movies and everything else—as distractions to keep us from thinking about God and really getting deep into Him. So a quiet time is when we separate ourselves from the world and get plugged in all over again. The Bible says, "Look at Jesus. He was the Son of God, and He got away to pray all the time."

> And when He had sent the multitudes away, He went up on a mountain by Himself to pray (Matthew 14:23).

> [He] said to the disciples, "Sit here while I go and pray over there" (Matthew 26:36).

> Very early the next morning, Jesus got up and went to a place where he could be alone and pray (Mark 1:35, *CEV*).

> Jesus went off to a mountain to pray, and he spent the whole night there (Luke 6:12, *CEV*).

Jesus would spend the whole night sometimes just praying to God, getting God to pour Himself out and getting filled up with God. He shared His heart with God, and then He went out the next day and chose all His disciples.

This whole idea of quiet times is not an option. If you want to change the world, you have to be filled with God. You can't go on what you were filled with yesterday. You can't rely on what happened at camp last summer or at church last Sunday. You have to get filled up again today, every day.

What issues that are important to you do you need to discuss with God today?

DANIEL'S COMMITMENT TO KEEP HIS QUIET TIMES

They could find no corruption in [Daniel], because he was trustworthy and neither corrupt nor negligent.

Daniel 6:4, *NIV*

Start off today by reading Daniel chapter 6.

Daniel was a young man who lived in a city called Babylon. He loved the Lord with all his heart and kept his quiet times strong every day. In fact, he prayed three times a day. God blessed his life so much that some of the other leaders were jealous because he had so much power. They tried to find something to accuse him of, but "they could find no corruption in him, because he was trustworthy and neither corrupt nor negligent" (Daniel 6:4, *NIV*).

Daniel was totally, wholeheartedly sold out to the Lord. He was a man of integrity who dealt with honesty and truth. Since the other leaders could find no valid means to dishonor him, they made a law that said if you prayed to anyone besides the king for thirty days, you would be thrown into the lions' den. The king, not really paying much attention to what he was doing, got suckered into making the law.

After Daniel found out about the law, he determined in his heart that he was going to do what was right—no matter what. Verse 10 records what Daniel was really made of: "Now when Daniel learned that the decree had been published, he went home to his upstairs room where the windows opened toward Jerusalem. Three times a day he got down on his knees and prayed, giving thanks to his God, just as he had done before" (*NIV*).

No matter what the circumstances, no matter what the situation is, stay focused on the Lord: *Leave the world behind, and make a commitment to have a quiet time every day*. Be able to say,

"People can do whatever they want to do to me. It doesn't matter. I love God with all my heart, and I'm going to do everything that I can to pursue Him with all that I am." Daniel knew that he might even die because he had chosen to keep his quiet times strong, but he didn't care.

If Daniel could be man enough and love God enough to keep his quiet times even in the face of death, can you have enough faith to stand up to the challenge and not let anything keep you from your quiet times? This is your chance to have the same kind of character as Daniel had and to say, "Whatever the world may try to do to me, people may say or do to me, I am going to love my God and go after Him with all my heart by keeping my quiet time every day." Would you make that commitment today and stick with it, no matter what?

Think about what might distract you from your quiet times. Make a list of these potential distractions and tell what you can do to avoid or eliminate each one.

DAY 7

COMMIT TO A LIFESTYLE OF PRAYER

When you pray, go into a room alone and close the door. Pray to your Father in private. He knows what is done in private, and he will reward you.

Matthew 6:6, *CEV*

God has given you the ability to hear from Him. To be strong, you have to let Him pour Himself into you right now, this morning. It cannot just be today; it has to be your lifestyle. It has to be so common that even your own family living with you would say the same thing about you that was said about Jesus: "He always got up and went somewhere to be alone and pray."

If somebody saw everything that you did, he would see your lifestyle habits. He would see that you always sneak away and find God. Some days you have to be desperate to accomplish it.

When I was going to college, I had roommates. I had to get up very quietly and sneak out of the room, because I didn't want to wake anybody up. I didn't want anyone to know that I was praying. I wanted to get the reward that only the Father could give. I just wanted to go off and get more of God in my life. I would stay out late at night just praying and walking around campus and looking at the stars. I wanted so much to hear the voice of God and know His heart and His ways.

Seeking God is like a hungering and a yearning from the bottom of your soul. Jesus said, "Blessed are those who hunger and thirst for righteousness, for they shall be filled" (Matthew 6:5). If you feel empty, you need to hunger and thirst for righteousness as you get up and have your quiet time. Cultivate a longing and a yearning for more of God, for purity, for life. Desire to hear His voice so big that He begins to fill you with more and more of Himself.

Too many Christians are empty. They have prayed, but they are still empty, because they are not hungering and thirsting for righteousness. As you seek God in your quiet times, you need to be hungry. Open up your Bible and say, "God, feed me today." As you read His Word, He will begin to fill you, and your life will get richer and fuller than you ever imagined possible.

I present to you a challenge this week. If you truly want to change the world, keep your relationship with Jesus alive. Cut off the dead, old, petrified nonrelationship you've had until now. Commit to having a living, exciting time with Jesus every day.

As a follower of Christ, I commit to keep my quiet times. I want to feed my hunger and thirst for God and His righteousness every day. I want my relationship with Jesus to be alive, and I want it to grow.

____________________________ ____________

Your Signature Date

WEEK 3

IT'S ALL ABOUT LOVE

LOVE STARTS WITH GOD

God is love. This is how God showed his love among us: He sent his one and only Son into the world that we might live through him.

1 John 4:8-9, *NIV*

Love starts with God, not with us. He's it. First John says God *is* love. There is no love outside of God—it originated with Him. He doesn't just *have* love to give—He *is* love. So when you get Him, you get love. And "this is love: Not that we loved God, but that he loved us" (1 John 4:10). He loved us first, before we ever knew love. He pours out His love to us and then we come alive. The more love we get from Him, the more love we have to give.

Love is the key to life. And it all starts with God loving us. We get filled with God Himself so that we can give others what He's given to us. If we don't have it, we can't give it. It's like a lamp—you have to plug it into the power source to get light. If it's not plugged in, no matter how hard it tries, it *will not* shine. Too many people are trying too hard to live the Christian life without being plugged into the power Source. You can only try so hard in your own efforts before you fail miserably and give up. Our own love doesn't last very long. But when we get plugged into the Source of love Himself, then it's His power that changes us and loves through us, and keeps on shining through the darkest dark!

Close your eyes for a minute and think about this: Have you been trying really hard lately, but still failing? Maybe you're not plugged into God's love yet. First John 3:1 says, "How great is the love the Father has *lavished* on us that we should be called children of God!" (*NIV*, emphasis added). And that is what we are!!

God has abundantly, generously, liberally and extravagantly rained down His love on you, His child, and called you His own. No matter who's rejected or neglected you, *He has not*. He receives you to Himself. Now open up your heart, and let that love pour deep into every crook and cranny, every memory, every hurt and every failure. Then watch God transform you into what you always wanted to be.

Write about a time when you felt rejected or neglected. How does knowing that God loves you—warts and all—make a difference?

___

___

___

___

___

___

___

___

___

___

___

___

LOVE GOD WITH YOUR ALL (PART 1: YOUR HEART)

You shall love the **L*ORD* *your God with all*** **your heart,** ***with all your soul, and with all your mind.***

Matthew 22:37 (emphasis added)

Matthew 22:37 records what Jesus called the first and greatest commandment.

God pours out all of His love on us, and then He commands us to love Him with it. Amazing, isn't it? You would think that every Christian would be doing this already. However, true followers take this command literally. In fact, they have had a complete transplant of their heart.

They have a kind of heart beating in them that is different from the one they had when they were born. They feel a passion to pursue God more than they pursue eating, because they've been changed by His love. They have a vibrant, living relationship with Him and refuse to get in a rut with it. They can feel the pulse of God inside their heart as they yearn to reach the rest of the world. They have surrendered every part of their heart to God, and they refuse to allow the world back in. God is the center of their heart, and they have rearranged all of their priorities. They see the world through different eyes now. They have different goals.

Think about this: Is there any part of your heart that you have not yet given over to God? The more of your heart you give to God, the more of His life He gives to you. Loving God with *all* of your heart requires that *He* has your whole heart, not just part of it. For everything you give to Him, He will give back something so much better! Remember, He's the originator of love and the biggest giver. You cannot out-give God.

Write down any parts of your heart you have withheld from God.

Now ask God to fill you with more love for Him so that you can love Him with every part of your heart.

LOVE GOD WITH YOUR ALL (PART 2: YOUR SOUL)

You shall love the Lord your God with all your heart, with all* your soul, *and with all your mind.

Matthew 22:37 (emphasis added)

God wants us to love Him with all that we are. The soul is made up of the mind, will and emotions. Loving God with all our soul is choosing to love Him with everything we do. We need to quit wasting our time occupying our minds and schedules with the distractions of the world and start getting mesmerized by God Himself!

Let the Creator of the universe give you His creative strategies and help you to plan exploits to change the world. Begin to make decisions about how you spend your time that will affect other people's lives eternally. Wrap everything you are into loving God. Be passionate about expressing your love for Him. Maybe you're an artist, a musician or a writer. Maybe God's gifted you with some other creative expression. Ask God how you can love Him with your creativity. He will begin to open doors for you as you love Him with all your soul.

Right now, think about how to get what you have into other people. Write down some creative ideas, strategies or plans to use your God-given gifts to show God's love to other people.

DAY 4

LOVE GOD WITH YOUR ALL (PART 3: YOUR MIND)

***You shall love the* L*ORD* *your God with all your heart, with all your soul, and with all* your mind.**

Matthew 22:37 (emphasis added)

What does loving God with all your mind mean? It means to love Him with what you think, to love Him in what you allow to go through your brain.

A lot of people say they love God with all their heart, but then they stop there. He doesn't want just your heart; He wants your mind, your will, your emotions—every part of you.

The world gives you plenty of things to think about, plenty of things that will distract you from thinking about the deep things of God. But if He really is the incredible God that He says He is—if He really has made the heavens and the earth and has done all of these mind-blowing things—He ought to be the One who totally lures your mind. He wants to be what you think about more than anything else.

Ask yourself, *If people could see all of my thoughts on an overhead projector, would they be able to tell that I really love God? Would that prove that I'm loving God with my mind?*

Take a minute or two to write down a few things that you can think about today to practice loving God with all your mind.

____

____

____

____

____

____

LOVE YOUR NEIGHBOR AS YOURSELF (PART 1: YOURSELF)

You shall love your neighbor **as yourself.**

Matthew 22:39 (emphasis added)

A lot of people focus on loving their neighbor, but they never think about loving themselves. Some people even think it's wrong to love yourself. But that's not what Jesus taught. He said that we need to love others *as* we love ourselves. "As" means "in the same way." So if you think that you're just an old rag to be used, abused and thrown out, then that's how you'll love other people.

If you don't love yourself, you won't be able to really love others. If this hits a nerve with you, go back to Day 1 of this week and meditate on God's love for you. If He loves you that much, you can love yourself. If He says you're worth loving, who are you to say you're not? If He has forgiven you, then you can forgive yourself. Is your judgment greater than God's? No, of course not! So don't hold something against yourself that God doesn't hold against you.

Choose to love yourself. Choose to forgive yourself. The more you meditate on God's love for you, the more you'll be able to love yourself. And the more you love yourself, the more you'll be able to love others.

Take a minute and think about anything that is keeping you from loving yourself. Write those things down.

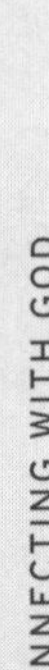

Have you ever asked God to forgive you of those things? If not, ask Him now to forgive you.

Now you stand forgiven before a holy God. He forgives you—now forgive yourself. Take another minute and ask Him to help you totally forgive yourself and love yourself the way He loves you.

DAY 6

LOVE YOUR NEIGHBOR AS YOURSELF (PART 2: YOUR NEIGHBOR)

You shall love **your neighbor** ***as yourself.***

Matthew 22:39 (emphasis added)

Love has to give in order for it to be love. Love cannot dwell alone. When God created the world, He couldn't keep it to Himself. He had to give because He *is* love. That was His challenge. So He created someone who could receive all the love in His heart: you and me. Now we have the same challenge as He had. We have been filled with so much love that we have to give it away—like He did.

This is where your challenge lies. Once you have given your all to love Him, He wants you to love the world. It is only in doing so that you will change it. The world cannot help being changed, for it has never seen love like that before.

Seek out neighbors. Be ready to seek out the harvest. Realize that it is just as important for others to have the gospel as it is for you to have it. Keep going out of your way to get it into the lives of other people. Be willing to leave your comfort zone and spend free time, even summer breaks, going to where the unreached people are. God will move you with His compassion to find and reach the world and bring the gospel to them. Find someone to give God's love to today.

Who are your neighbors? Read Luke 10:30-37. What specific actions can you take this week to love your neighbors?

DAY 7

COMMIT TO FOLLOW THE MOST EXCELLENT WAY

And now I will show you the most excellent way.

1 Corinthians 12:31, *NIV*

Read 1 Corinthians 13, "The Love Chapter."

Paul said that we can have all kinds of spiritual gifts, the highest form of faith that moves mountains or even charity, but if we don't have love, all that means absolutely nothing. That's pretty mind-blowing when you think about it. If you saw a man give everything he had to the poor, you would think he was incredible; or if you saw a woman get burned at the stake for her faith, you would think she was a pretty awesome person. But the Bible says that without love, even those kinds of good works gain nothing for us. We've got to have the God kind of love in our lives. The God kind of love is the kind that loves no matter what we get in return. God loved you and me like that. Before we loved Him, before we gave Him anything, He reached out and He loved us unconditionally. We didn't deserve it, but He loved us anyway. That's real love.

God is love—He doesn't just have love to give; He *is* love. So take a minute right now and ask God to fill you with more of Himself today—that unconditional, unexpecting love—so that you can begin to live "the most excellent way" of life.

As a follower of Christ, I commit to follow God's way, the way of love. I will love God with all my heart, soul and mind; and I will love myself in the same way that I love my neighbor.

______________________________ ______________

Your Signature Date

WEEK 4

TRANSFORM YOUR MIND, TRANSFORM YOUR LIFE

DAY 1

RENEW YOUR MIND

Do not be conformed to this world, but be transformed by the renewing of your mind, that you may prove what is that good and acceptable and perfect will of God.

Romans 12:2

Let's talk about loving God with your mind and really committing your mind to God.

When you get saved, you commit your heart to God. You love Him with all your heart, and that's great. Now you need to say, "Lord, I want You to affect my mind. I don't want You just to affect this invisible heart of mine. I want You to begin to change the way I think." As He changes the way you think, your life will be absolutely revolutionized, because it will change the way you live.

Take five minutes and memorize Romans 12:2 right now. Be transformed by the renewing of your mind.

Some people pray, "God, please change my life. Please change what I do. I'm so sorry." Let me tell you right now that God has already given you the ability to change your life in every area, and He has told you what to do. You say, "Lord, I love You with all my heart." He says, "Good. Now I want you to love Me with all your mind." The way to do that is to put godly things in your mind. He says that your life will be transformed by renewing your mind.

Your mind has been corroded over the years. You live in a world that is full of sin, full of garbage, full of hatred and evil. Everywhere you turn—whether it be radio, newspapers, magazines, movies, TV or the Internet—is sin, sin, sin. These things have been crammed down your throat since you were born. But now you have really come alive, because you've been born again. You have a new spirit, a new heart. God wants the newness of your heart to affect your mind so that the way you live will be affected.

Maybe you've prayed for your mind to become clean, and then you've gone out and thought something bad. You may think, *Oh, I guess I didn't really mean it.* Sure, you did. It's just that your mind has been brainwashed with a lot of wrong ideas ever since you were a child. Now you need to renew your mind.

What does renewing your mind really mean? It means to begin thinking God's thoughts instead of the world's thoughts. Think about truth instead of lies. Feed your brain with the stuff that God thinks instead of wasting time thinking about what you saw on a billboard, a bathroom wall or a television program. Your life is changed when you begin to think differently, and the way you live is transformed by renewing your mind. Make a conscious decision to put in your mind only things that are going to push you to grow toward God.

Think about what you fill your mind with. What movies and TV programs are worth watching? What magazines would be good to read? What music and/or radio shows would be good to listen to? (Maybe do some research: Get started by checking out Christian websites that review various kinds of media and by talking to your youth pastor.)

THE BATTLE IS IN YOUR MIND

Whatever things are true, whatever things are noble, whatever things are just, whatever things are pure, whatever things are lovely, whatever things are of good report, if there is any virtue and if there is anything praiseworthy—meditate on these things.

Philippians 4:8

One goal of the Christian life is to live as much like Jesus as you possibly can. You need to get rid of the garbage in your life and change the way you live so that when people look at you, they get a glimpse of Jesus. You have to put to death the things of the flesh—sinful things—and take on godly and pure habits.

We talked yesterday about your being transformed by the renewing of your mind. You can change the things you do by changing the way you think. That's because your battle is not with the things that you do; the battle happens in your mind. If you win the battle in your mind, you win the battle in your actions.

Paul described this problem in Romans 7:21-23:

> I find then a law, that evil is present with me, the one who wills to do good. For I delight in the law of God according to the inward man. But I see another law in my members, warring against the law of my mind, and bringing me into captivity to the law of sin which is in my members.

Your mind is the go-between. In your heart, you want to do good and holy things. But your body does ungodly things. Your mind is like the referee and hates the things your body does. If you force your mind to think on whatever is true and lovely and worthy of praise, then you will do things that are true and lovely and worthy of praise.

The battleground is your mind. If you are determined to live like Jesus and you are determined to be like Him, then you have to make sure that your thoughts are transformed, that the way you think is more the way God thinks. You do that by cramming the Bible in your heart and your mind. The battle in your mind is waged every day. If you want to be transformed more and more every day, then you need to start every day by reading and meditating on the Scriptures; that is what will help you become strong so that you win the battle.

A great place to start winning the battle in your mind is by memorizing Philippians 4:8. Do that now. (And then, of course, record your memorization in the back of the book!) Think about this verse all day today. Win the battle that is in your mind by keeping God's Word in the forefront of your mind.

Think about the battle David fought with Goliath (see 1 Samuel 17) or the battle Joshua fought for Jericho (see Joshua 6). How did David and Joshua win each battle? How can you show that you rely on God to help you win the battle in your mind?

____

____

____

____

____

____

____

____

DAY 3

HOW TO WIN CONTROL OF YOUR THOUGHT LIFE (PART 1)

We demolish arguments and every pretension that sets itself up against the knowledge of God, and we take captive every thought to make it obedient to Christ.

2 Corinthians 10:5, *NIV*

We are talking about how to live a life that is totally committed to following Christ and living like He did.

We talked yesterday about the fact that the battle for change is in your mind. Today, we're going to begin talking about how to win that battle. Second Corinthians 10:5 describes exactly what to do. You have to face the fact right now that if you are going to win the battle in your mind, you are going to have to *do* something. And today is the day to start taking action.

In today's Scripture, you're told to "demolish arguments and every pretension [thought] that sets itself up against the knowledge of God." You demolish anything that pops in your mind that acts like it is more important than God or that is an adversary to God.

What does the Bible mean by this? You have to compare anything that comes in your head to the Scriptures. For example, if a sinful thought comes into your mind (*Wow! I want all that money!*), you compare that thought to the Scriptures ("Don't be greedy"—see Luke 12:15-31). If that thought is setting itself up against the knowledge of God, it needs to be destroyed.

The point is, you don't let every thought that comes into your brain stay in your brain. Some people think, *I don't have a choice. Whatever I think just pops in there.* Well, you don't always have the choice in the first moment that it enters, but you do have the choice about whether or not it stays. That's what this Scripture is talking about: You demand of yourself that thoughts contrary to God be destroyed.

We're so used to just letting whatever thoughts come into our head be the things we think about. But we do have a choice, and whatever we think about will become our actions and will become who we are.

Today as thoughts come to your mind, begin to recognize if they are of God or not. If you're not sure, find out what the Bible says about that thought; and if it doesn't agree with God, don't allow it to stay in your mind.

List two or three sinful thoughts you've had trouble with lately.

____

____

____

____

____

____

____

____

Now draw a line through each one, and as you draw each line, wipe out that thought from your mind. Destroy it. As you do, you'll begin to win the battle.

HOW TO WIN CONTROL OF YOUR THOUGHT LIFE (PART 2)

We demolish arguments and every pretension that sets itself up against the knowledge of God, and we take captive every thought to make it obedient to Christ.

2 Corinthians 10:5, *NIV*

I want to further talk about the verse: "We take captive every thought to make it obedient to Christ." This means that you grab hold of every thought that comes to mind. In other words, you don't just let whatever flies into your brain stay in there. You grab it, and you make it obedient to Christ. If it's not obedient, you demolish it. If it's obedient, you let it stay.

The point is, you have a choice about what goes on in your mind. The more you think sinful thoughts, the more you'll do sinful things. But the more you allow God's Word to infiltrate your mind, the more you'll win the battle over what you do. The more you think holy thoughts, the more you'll do holy things.

It's your choice about whether or not to let a sinful thought continue to take root in your brain and go into your heart. You can choose to demolish it. Today is your chance to demolish ungodly thoughts. But you can't demolish them just by saying, "I don't want them in my brain." You must replace them with something holy.

It's like this: If I said, "Don't think about little pink monkeys right now," that's all you would be able to think about. But if I said to think about big green elephants, with their big green ears and big green trunks, it would be easy not to think of the little pink monkeys because you would be focused on the big green elephants.

It's the same with renewing your mind. If you want to stop thinking bad thoughts, instead of saying, *I won't think about it*—

I just won't think about it, you focus your mind on what the Word of God says and it will literally demolish the wrong thoughts.

That's why it's so important to take your Scripture with you every day so that you can have the Word of God with you wherever you go. Every time you get a sinful thought, take your Scripture out of your pocket, quote the Scripture in Jesus' name and put your foot down. In that very moment, you demolish that sinful thought with the Word of God. Today, I want you to take 2 Corinthians 10:5 with you all day. See how many times you can literally demolish evil thoughts that come into your mind. You, as a follower of Christ, have to take your mind back and let it be a seedbed for the Word of God.

Remember those two or three sinful thoughts you wrote down and wiped out of your mind yesterday? Today, list a Scripture to replace each one. (For example, if one of your thoughts had to do with wanting some expensive designer clothes, write down Luke 12:23.) If you need help finding passages on different topics, talk with a parent or your youth pastor.

DAY 5

DEALING WITH SPECIFIC BATTLES

His delight is in the law of the Lord, and in His law he meditates day and night.

Psalm 1:2

I trust you had a victorious day yesterday demolishing and taking captive the thoughts that go against the Word of God. Today, we want to deal in a very practical way with a couple of examples of the battles you are going to have to win. For example, maybe you have had a problem with anger. You get mad; you get ticked off; maybe you've cussed at people in the past. Now you're saying that you want to be like Jesus. You know that kind of rage and anger is not like the Lord, so you're going to do something about it.

Remember, the battle starts in your mind. It's not just saying, "I'm not going to get mad." You have to change the way you think. When you change the way you think, you change the way you act.

You can find some Scriptures that pertain to anger. Ephesians 4:26-27 says, " 'In your anger do not sin': Do not let the sun go down while you are still angry, and do not give the devil a foothold" (*NIV*). You look at Scriptures that say things like, "He who holds his tongue is wise" (Prov. 10:19, *NIV*), and you take the Scriptures with you all day long. You begin your quiet time by meditating and chewing on those Scriptures so that when you launch your day, you are full of the Word of God.

You already have a stronghold in your mind that says, "I know I am going to live the way God wants me to live." Then every time you are tempted to sound off in anger, you pull out the Scripture card and think, *I'm going to be angry, yet I will not sin. I will not let my anger control me.* That moment is your opportunity to change the way you think, which will change the way you act.

Here's another example. Maybe someone in your life has really done you wrong. You know you have to forgive the person, but you don't really want to. You're mad at the person, and you know you should forgive him or her, but you don't want to, so you stay in the battle that's going on in your mind.

You need to change the way you think. Read Matthew 18:21-35. Jesus was asked, "How often shall my brother sin against me, and I forgive him?" (v. 21). He said you should forgive "up to seventy times seven" (v. 22). Jesus then went on to tell the parable of the unmerciful servant. This story describes how a master forgave one of his servants a huge debt, but that same servant refused to forgive someone who owed him a much smaller debt (see vv. 23-35).

You begin to meditate and chew on that all day long. Then make a decision to forgive, even though you don't feel like it. You do it because you know it's right. You continue to chew on the forgiveness Scriptures, and God gives you the power to forgive and gives you the freedom to know what it's like to really forgive.

If you're angry with someone or if you need to forgive someone, describe the situation.

Write down the Scripture you can use to fight the battle in your mind.

You will win today, and your actions will change as well!

DAY 6

SET YOUR MIND ON THINGS ABOVE

Since, then, you have been raised with Christ, set your hearts on things above, where Christ is seated at the right hand of God. Set your minds on things above, not on earthly things.

Colossians 3:1-2, *NIV*

The Bible exhorts you to set your mind and heart "on things above." The Bible says that you can choose what you set your mind on. You could set it on the things of the world, you could set it on other people, you could set it on entertainment, or you could set it on having fun, but the Bible says to set your mind on things above. The best way to set your mind on things above is to get your mind into the Word of God.

I want you to notice the word "set." It is your choice to set your mind on whatever you want to. The Bible says you are an alien and stranger in this world (see 1 Peter 2:11, *NIV*), so don't just wear a Christian label. Let God stir up your heart and your mind. Set your mind to aggressively go after the things of God.

Today, you can choose what you will set your mind on: the things of the world or the things above. What are you choosing to set your mind on in your everyday life at school or at work? What are you focusing on? Are you living for what is here on earth and just having a little quiet time in the morning? Or are you setting your mind on things of God throughout the day? Are you saying to yourself, *God, I want You to use me. Lord, I want to know You. I want to think Your thoughts. I want to know Your ways*?

Setting your mind on the things above basically means choosing to bombard yourself with the truth, with what is right, with what is holy. For so long, you've lived in this world and been brainwashed with lies. Now is the time for you to immerse yourself in the truth—it's time to cram the truth down your throat.

This reminds me of when I had just turned on to the Lord. My father and I would go out to work. I would turn the radio station to listen to preachers, and he would turn it to listen to some music. I'd turn it back to preachers. Finally, he'd say, "Son, you just need balance! You need balance in your life." I thought for a while about what he said. I didn't say this to him, but I thought, *You know, Dad, you're right. I do need balance. And I've had so much garbage crammed down my throat from the devil and the world that I'm going to need the Word of God in my mind and in my heart 24 hours a day for the next 20 years just to get balanced. I need to get my mind set on things above.*

List a few worldly things you have a tendency to let your mind dwell on (a person you think is cute, a violent video game, a song that uses garbage language—whatever).

___

___

___

___

___

___

___

___

___

Today, any time your mind starts to wander, use Colossians 3:1-2 as a reminder to get your mind set on things above.

DAY 7

COMMIT TO HAVING THE MIND OF CHRIST

"No eye has seen, no ear has heard, no mind has conceived what God has prepared for those who love him" but God has revealed it to us by his Spirit. . . . We have the mind of Christ.

1 Corinthians 2:9-10,16, *NIV*

The Bible is describing a mind that is totally committed to God. This is what you can expect. First of all, it says, "No eye has seen, no ear has heard"; no one has even thought of what God has prepared for us. The average Joe walking down the street could never imagine how incredible the stuff is that God has prepared for us.

However, verse 10 says that "God has revealed it to us by his Spirit." In other words, God has revealed by His Spirit the incredible, amazing things that He wants to do in us, through us and to us. But only people who have His Spirit are going to get this revelation.

Then the Bible says that "we have the mind of Christ." This means that as you begin to put more and more of the Bible in your mind, you think more like God because the things He said are rolling around in your mind. As you train your mind to think the way God does, you get the mind of Christ. God will speak some very incredible things to you regarding what He wants to do in your life and through your life. He'll explain to you how He wants to use you to change the world and set people free, to change whole villages, communities, states and countries. God will speak to you and tell you how He wants to use you, because your mind has been trained; it is now like the mind of Christ.

Some Christians wonder why God never speaks to them. The problem is that they haven't trained their minds to think like God thinks. Maybe God is speaking to them, but they don't understand His words because they still think like the world thinks. Sure, they committed their heart to God, but they never committed their mind. As a result, the things God wants to do in their lives are still a mystery to them. They continue to think, *Maybe God will lead me someday*. Life has become a vague journey for them.

I want to encourage you to make a commitment, not just for this week and not just for the duration of this devotional book, but for at least the rest of your teen years: to commit your mind to God, to choose to focus on things above. As you do this, you will begin to get the mind of Christ and hear the voice of God. It's a radical difference from the way the average person thinks.

If you're going to change the world, you have to begin by changing yourself. You'll be amazed as you watch yourself become more and more like God. As you begin to change the world, you will change it more into the way God wants it because you can think the way God thinks. He has changed your mind and your heart. As a result, He has changed your actions, and you will change the world.

As a follower of Christ, I herby commit my mind to the things of God. I commit to regularly memorize and meditate on Scripture. I will cram the Word in my brain, I will take captive any thoughts that go against the will of God and I will set my mind on things above so that I can have the mind of Christ and change the world like He wants me to.

______________________________ ______________

Your Signature Date

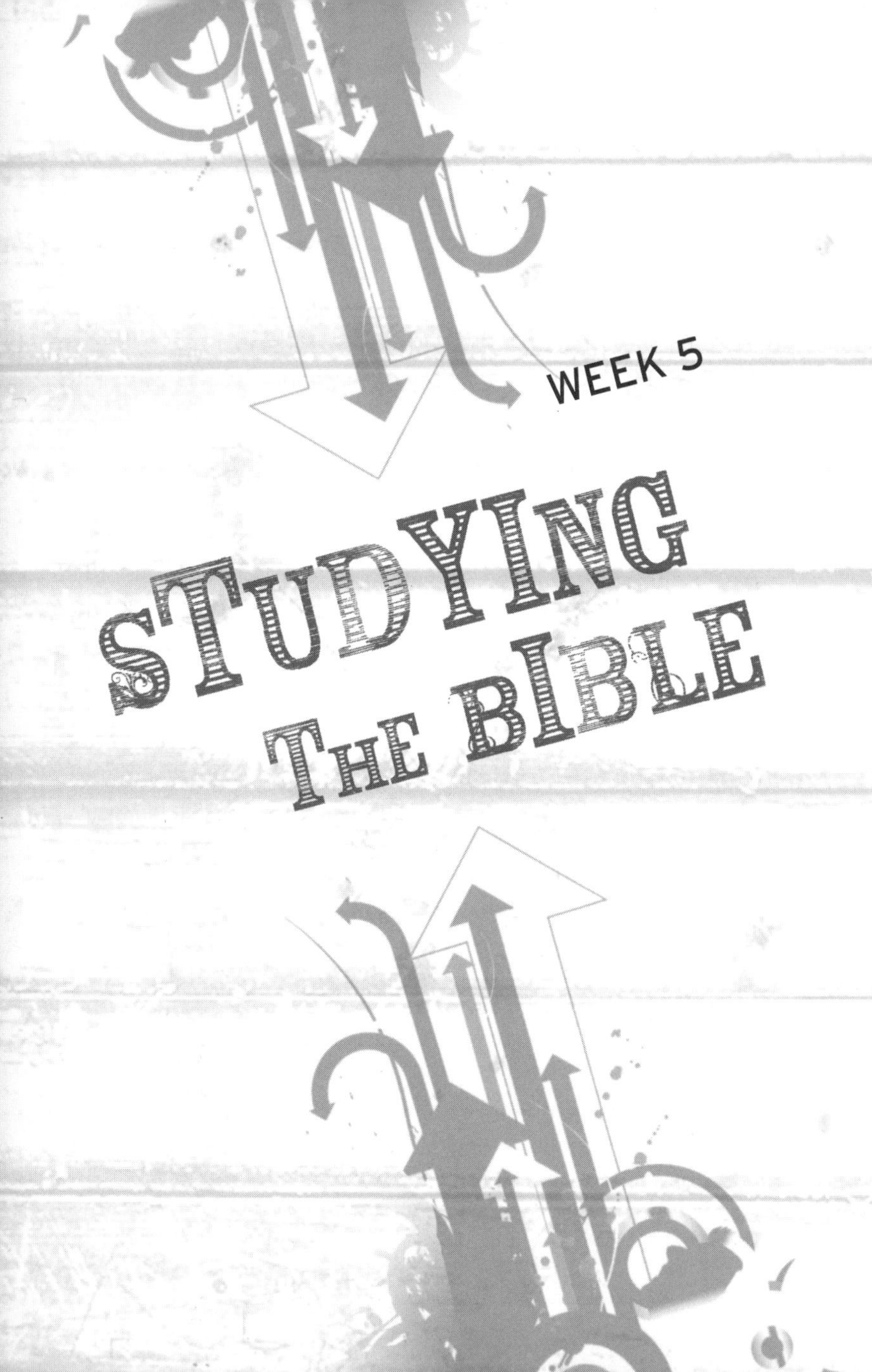

WEEK 5

STUDYING THE BIBLE

WHAT THE WORD IS

In the beginning was the Word, and the Word was with God, and the Word was God. He was in the beginning with God. . . . The Word became flesh and dwelt among us.

John 1:1-2,14

The Bible says that the Word was in the very beginning, that the Word was with God, and that the Word actually was God. It is important for you to study the Bible, which is the Word of God, on a regular basis. I want you to really understand what the Word of God is all about.

As a follower of Christ, you can't just haphazardly "sort of" get into the Bible; you've got to get into it with all your heart and soul. A word is not merely something that somebody says. The essence of a word is an expression of a thought.

Whenever God speaks something, He expresses what He already thought about beforehand. When you read that the Word was with God and the Word was God, you see that what God was thinking, He began to speak about. And whenever God spoke, amazing things happened.

He said, "Let there be light," and there was the sun. He said, "Let there be earth . . . plants . . . stars," and they all came to be (see Genesis 1:6-15). God thought it, He said it, and then an amazing thing happened: it just exploded. That is how powerful God's words are.

The Bible goes on to say that the Word became flesh and dwelt among us. In other words, what God was thinking became form—in this case, flesh. We know this is His Son, Jesus Christ. Colossians 1:15 says that Jesus is "the image of the invisible God." If you want to know what God is thinking, look at Jesus. He is the expressed image of the invisible God. He is the Word made flesh.

When you read God's Word, you'll begin to understand what is going on in God's mind, what He is thinking about. Ninety percent of all the questions you would ever want to ask God are answered right in His Word. You've just *got* to realize how valuable the Bible is.

This week we are going to be talking about getting the Word of God in your life on a regular basis. This is directly linked to transforming your mind, just as we talked about last week. Now instead of your mind being committed to the world, it's committed to the Word. To be committed to the Word, you've got to really study it. As you do, your spirit will be fed, and you will grow into a strong person of God.

As a follower of Christ, you've got to be serious about really getting to know God. The more you get to know His Word, the more you get to know His thoughts, and the more you get to know Him and what He's really like.

Take some time today to memorize and meditate on today's Scripture. Really think about God's Word. Realize that these are God's thoughts you're memorizing. What He's thinking—what's going through His mind and His heart—is what you are memorizing as you take the Scriptures to heart.

You have unlimited access to the Word (Jesus) and to God's Word (the Bible). How do you plan to get to know both better?

THE VALUE OF READING THE WORD

All scripture is God-breathed and is useful for teaching, rebuking, correcting and training in righteousness, so that the man of God may be thoroughly equipped for every good work.

2 Timothy 3:16-17, *NIV*

Take three minutes and memorize 2 Timothy 3:16-17 right now.

This passage describes the fact that all Scripture is inspired by God—it came out of His heart. It's valuable for several specific things in your life. First of all, it's useful for teaching. The more you read the Word, the more God will begin to teach your heart. Teach you what? God's Word will teach you how to live in this world, how to be successful, how to prosper, how to have vision, how to have a dream, how to fulfill your dreams, how to manage finances, how to conduct friendships and other relationships, how to deal with marriage, and how to be the person God wants you to be. The Word teaches you how to live.

The world teaches you how to live in a wrong way. Anything good the world happens to teach happens because it lines up with the Word of God. Why try to sift through all the junk in the world? Just go straight to the Word. You will learn principles that will teach you how to live and how to pull your life together.

Name a couple of areas of your life that you would like God to really teach you about.

____

____

____

____

____

____

____

God's Word is also valuable for rebuking and correcting. There may be things in your life that need to be rebuked and corrected. As you read the Word of God, you will be instructed and corrected; you will be shown the right way to do things.

You'll read a Scripture—a story or parable Jesus told or something in the Old Testament—and all of a sudden you'll go, *Wow! That's happening in my life.* That's exactly what Paul meant in 2 Corinthians 3:16: "When one turns to the Lord, the veil is taken away."

Maybe you'll feel rebuked by the Lord: "Hey, [put your name in here!], you need to get this part of your life together." When you feel that, you should say, "Okay, Lord, I'm listening." Then repent and commit to memorize that Scripture and meditate on it until your life lines up with the Word.

The verse also says that the Word will train you in righteousness. This world trains you in unrighteousness. It teaches you in the way everyone lives and the examples of an unholy, ungodly, unrighteous life. The world's ways may be fun and look good at first, but that way leads to destruction and misery. The Word of God teaches you with positive examples, encouragement, rebukes and exhortation how to live righteously in an unrighteous world.

God is expecting you to do a lot of good works in this world. As you cram the Word of God down your throat, He will equip you to do all the incredible things He wants you to do to change the world.

Name a couple of areas of your life that you would like God to help you correct.

____

____

____

____

____

____

Write out 2 Timothy 3:16-17 on an index card and carry it with you as you deal with areas you feel God wants to correct.

UNDERSTANDING THE WORD

Incline your ear to wisdom, and apply your heart to understanding.

Psalm 2:2

When you read the Bible, make sure that it doesn't become just another book. It must not become the obligatory "I've got to read a couple of chapters today because of my commitment" thing. You want to really look for how God wants to speak to you through specific things in His Word. Let me give you a couple of things to look for every day as you read.

First of all, as you get ready to read any book in the Bible, read the introduction to it. Most Bibles you buy today will have a little bit of an introduction to tell you about the author, why he wrote the book, when it was written, and so forth. That can help you better understand what is going on in the book you are about to read.

Then as you begin reading, think about the people the book was written to. Ultimately it was written to you because, by the Holy Spirit, God speaks to all of us. However, take time to think about the original audience. Did Moses write the book? Who were the people he wrote it to? Did Paul write it? Who was he addressing? These questions and their answers can help you understand why the author said some of the things he said.

For example, 1 and 2 Corinthians were written by Paul to the church in Corinth, which was living in sin. He was telling them specific things about how to fight the sin there.

The next question to ask is, Why did the author write it? Did Paul write his letters because he was bored in jail, or was he writing to get a specific point across? If you understand the author's purpose, you'll understand more of what you read.

For example, turn to the book of Luke. In chapter 1, he states that he wrote that book to give a very accurate picture of who Jesus was (see Luke 1:3). He was not writing to everybody; he was writing to his friend. He wrote a letter of Jesus' life to a friend, and we ended up getting that letter and publishing the book of Luke in the Bible.

The final question to ask is, What did it mean to the original audience? Sometimes we find a verse or passage, take it out of context and make it say something that the author never meant to say. Try to put yourself in the mindset of the people to whom the book was written. Think of what was going through their minds the first time they heard all the words. As you think about what the words meant to them, you may be able to better understand more of what they mean for you.

Why don't you try this today? Go back and read the introduction to whatever book of the Bible you were reading today. When you read the chapter you are on, think about who wrote it, the people it was written to, why the author wrote it and what it meant to the original audience.

What Bible book are you reading right now? Who wrote it? Who did he intend to read it or hear it? Why did he write it? What do you think it meant to the original audience?

By answering these questions for every Bible book you read, you'll be amazed at the insights you'll get.

GETTING THE MOST OUT OF THE WORD

I will meditate on Your precepts, and I will contemplate Your ways. I will delight myself in Your statutes; I will not forget Your word.

Psalm 119:15-16

Today we are going to discuss some very specific things that will help you get a lot out of the Bible as you read it.

We are talking about having a relationship with God. The problem is, how do you have a relationship with someone you can't see? How do you get closer to somebody if you can't see how close you are now? How do you know somebody well? After all, isn't that what a relationship is about?

Think about one of your friends. How can you tell whether you really know a friend? Is it because you are physically close? You could sit next to your friend every day in geometry and not really know him or her at all. Knowing someone is not about being physically close.

How do you get to know God? Think about how you got to know a close friend. If you know someone really well and somebody else accuses your friend of something you know is not true, you can say, "No way. I know that's not true." You know it's a lie because you know that person; you know she would never do that.

So what does it really mean to know a person? It means you know her character, what she's like on the inside, what she's made of. You know whether she would ever do the things she's been accused of.

That is exactly what I'm talking about when I say you need to get to know God. He's invisible, so you can't see Him, but that doesn't mean you can't get to know Him. Getting to know God means getting to know His character, His personality.

David talks about this in the psalms. He says, "I will meditate on your precepts, and contemplate Your ways." He goes on all the way through chapter 119. He says, "I think about Your ways, Your principles, and Your statutes." In other words, when God does something, He always does it the same way. That is what a principle is. You learn to say, "Lord, I love Your precepts. The more I get to know Your laws, the more I get to know who You are really like."

Reading the Bible is not just going through it and reading a verse here or a story there. It's actually going on a *quest for God*. Every single day, wake up saying, "God, I love Your principles. I love Your precepts. I want Your ways."

In every chapter of the Bible you read, you should be asking this huge question: What can I learn about God's character? Ask yourself, *What can I learn about the way He does things? How can the way He treated somebody or the way He did something be a guiding principle in my life? What does the fact that He delivered someone from his enemies mean to me?*

This morning as you dive into the Word and read a chapter or two, ask yourself, *What can I learn about God's character, His nature and His principles?* If each day you can grab hold of just one principle of what God is really like, you will have the most incredible life, because you will be getting to know Him better and better every day.

After your Bible reading today, write down something you learned about God's character.

MEDITATE ON THE WORD

Oh, how I love Your law! It is my meditation all the day.

Psalm 119:97

As we learned yesterday, the author of Psalm 119:15-16 loved the Word of God. He meditated and chewed on it, and he delighted in chewing on the Word: "Your testimonies also are my delight and my counselors" (v. 24). He repeated this thought again in verse 48—"My hands also I will lift up to Your commandments, which I love, and I will meditate on Your statutes"—and yet again in verse 97, the verse for today.

Meditation is not the same as memorization. When you memorize something, you just quote it. When you meditate on something, you chew on it and you chew on it, just like a cow chews its cud. Cows have a stomach with four compartments. When they eat, they chew their food only enough to swallow it. It's broken down some and later coughed up. Then it's chewed on some more and swallowed again.

That is exactly what you're doing when you meditate. You're chewing on God's Word and chewing on it; it's stirring you up and you keep chewing on it and chewing on it. When you've chewed on it long enough, you begin to be able to digest it, just like a cow does. After doing this for a while, it becomes alive to you. It's not just a boring little Scripture; it's real because you've chewed on it enough for it to sink into your mind. So the question for each day is, *What Scripture are you chewing on?*

The Bible describes this concept in a different way in Ephesians 5:26. It talks about washing your mind with the water of the truth. All the brainwashing the world has done to you begins to get washed away, and your mind gets cleaned up. It's a choice that you make; you don't accidentally get washed with the Word. You've got to choose, just like the author of Psalm 119 did, to meditate and meditate and chew and chew on one Scripture and let it really sink down into your heart and mind.

Meditating on God's Word is a great habit to get into because then what you read isn't just another story. It's life for you. It's real food for you that triggers your heart to believe that it's true. The scales fall from your eyes, and God's Word sets you free. It comes alive to you.

Choose a Scripture today—maybe one of the Scriptures that you have already memorized during this study. Chew on it like you have never chewed on anything before in your life. Every spare moment you have, chew and chew and chew, repeat it again and again to yourself, over and over. Then watch and see what God does in your heart today!

Come back to this page before you go to bed tonight, and answer the following two questions: *What Scripture did you choose? What did God do in your heart today?*

DAY 6

APPLY THE WORD TO YOUR LIFE

For the Word of God is living and active. Sharper than any double-edged sword, it penetrates even to dividing soul and spirit, joints and marrow; it judges the thoughts and attitudes of the heart.

Hebrews 4:12, *NIV*

The Bible describes the kinds of things the Word of God can do in your life. It says that the Word of God is not just some boring book that somebody wrote; it's living and it's active. That's the thing the world doesn't understand about the Bible: *It's alive and active*.

If you meditated, really meditated, on the Word yesterday as we talked about, you probably discovered how alive and active the Word is. It's so alive that it can pierce your heart, deal with things in your life and change your life like nothing else can. As you learn to apply specific Scriptures to your life in areas where you're struggling, you're confused, you're overcoming sin, you begin to realize how active His Word is, how alive it really can be.

Every day as you read a portion of the Scriptures and begin to discover who God is and what He's like, ask yourself several questions: *What is this saying to me today? How can I apply to my life what God is saying here? If I were there living in the time this Scripture was written, what would I need to take into my heart and ask God to change in me?*

The Word of God is also living and active in areas of your life that you know you need to change but don't know how to. Remember our discussion earlier about getting transformed by the renewing of your mind? You cram the Bible in your mind about that particular issue, and it begins to change your mind and then your actions.

I've talked to many people with specific problems in their lives who have gone to counselors to work out their problems. They have spent a lot of money but haven't gotten any answers. They get so discouraged because they can't get over their problems. Then, all of a sudden, they get into the Bible and because the Bible is living and active, their lives are changed. Remember that the Bible is not just another philosophy or pop-psychology book. It's the Word of God. You get enough of it in your life and it changes you; it literally changes you.

Believe me—I've seen them, and I've talked with them. They get set free by getting into the Word and letting God change their lives by His free gift. Of course, there are many people who are helped by counseling, but it is important to remember that it's the truth, not psychology, that sets you free.

I want you to take a moment and list some areas of your life that you know need to change. God probably has spoken to you in the past about them. Maybe they're sinful thoughts, sinful desires or sinful actions. Take a moment and write them here. Just concentrate on the problem areas first—we will fill in the Scriptures in a minute.

Problem Area

______

______

______

Scripture(s)

______

______

Problem Area

______

______

______

Scripture(s)

______

______

Problem Area

Scripture(s)

Now look in your Bible and find one or more Scriptures that apply to each of these areas. If you have trouble coming up with applicable verses, go to a concordance or ask your pastor or somebody else who is trustworthy for a Scripture that will tell you how to deal with that area.

Choose one of the problem areas you listed above, and on a card write out the Scripture(s) you found to go with it; then take the card with you today. Meditate on the Scripture, chew on it and let it become alive to you so that you can apply it to the problem area of your life. Watch the transformation begin!

COMMIT TO STUDY THE WORD

The word of the Lord endures forever.

1 Peter 1:25

As a follower of Christ, you've got to realize that you have to be a living, breathing Word machine. Devour the Word of God. Let it transform your brain. Cram it down your throat, and let it begin to stir up your insides.

I don't care whether you are 13, 15 or 18 years old. Age doesn't matter. It's time right now to change the way you think: Think more like God. You need to live more like Him as His Word becomes alive inside you

Another essential element to stand strong in as a follower is to read the Bible all the way through on a regular basis. Don't just open the Bible and say, "This must be where God wants me to read today." You need to read through the whole Bible again and again and again.

You don't have to go through the whole Bible this week, but you do need to begin now. Decide that you're going to read one book a week or a month or whatever—*something*—just set a goal now.

Do something to really get the Word inside you. Start at the beginning (Genesis 1:1) and go all the way through to the end (Revelation 22:21). It might take you a year or two, but you've got to make the decision right now not to be an airhead Christian who knows only a little about the Bible. Dive into it and really know it. Don't think you know it because you heard your pastor preach it to you. You need to know it for yourself.

You need to know the order of events. Did King David come before King Solomon or after King Jehoshaphat? Did Moses come before or after David? Learn the history and the order of how God did things, and you will learn about the character and nature of God.

There are so many systematic Bible studies out there you can do. Some you can finish the whole Bible in one year. You can find a system you like.

One great way is to read both the Old Testament and the New Testament at the same time. Begin by reading one chapter in Genesis and one in Matthew.

You may get so excited you want to read five chapters in one book. That's okay, just as long as you keep the commitment to read every day. You can also read through the psalms and proverbs as a part of your daily reading.

If you're going to change the world, you've got to be aggressively into the Word of God and make the commitment to read and study it every day.

As a follower of Christ, I commit to seek out the character of God by studying the Word of God. I will meditate on it and let it become alive to me. I will systematically read through the Bible so that I get all the way through the Bible at least one time during my teen years.

______________________________ ______________

Your Signature Date

WEEK 6

ACCOUNTABILITY FRIENDSHIPS

WHAT AN ACCOUNTABILITY FRIENDSHIP IS ALL ABOUT

A friend loves at all times, and a brother is born for adversity.

Proverbs 17:17

What is an accountability friend? The definition of "accountability" is "obliged to account for one's acts, being responsible, capable of being accounted for." Having an accountability friend is letting someone else be in a position to hear your account of your life.

An accountability friend or partner is someone you trust to love you at all times—the good times as well as the bad times, when you are on rocky ground and when you are sailing victoriously.

One of the problems often encountered by a person who commits his or her life to Christ is that the person continues to surround him- or herself with people who do not love the Lord. The new follower of Christ then feels as if he or she can't be him- or herself around other people and really let them know everything going on in his or her life. If something is done to really blow the new follower's walk with God, it is kept quiet, and the person begins to develop a list of secret sins.

An accountability friend will love you whether you do right or wrong, but such a friend loves you too much to let you do bad things and do nothing about it. Instead, this friend will kick you in the backside and help you get your act back together.

As a follower of Christ, you cannot afford to be a Lone Ranger Christian. Christianity is not about coming forward to the altar, crying and praying, and hoping you can change your life by yourself. It's about getting locked in with other people who have the same fire and passion to change the world.

Christianity is about locking arms and hearts with people and saying, "We love each other too much to let each other backslide.

We love each other too much to let each other get into sin and not say something about it." It's about getting in each other's face and helping each other go for God.

If you try to ride off like a Lone Ranger Christian, you make yourself a really easy target for the devil to pick off. You must lock arms and lock hearts with several other people who are committed and accountable to each other and say, "If you see anything in my life that doesn't look like Jesus, I want you to tell me about it. I want so much to look like Jesus, and I don't want anything to accidentally get in my life that I don't deal with." That is what accountability friendship is all about.

A real friend will love you at all times, even though she might see something that is not going very well in your life. She'll love you enough to tell you about what's going on. It's not about judging each other; it's about being committed in good times and bad.

Meditate on Proverbs 17:17 today.

What areas in your life do you need to be held accountable for?

Begin to pray and ask God for an accountability friend or two who can really push you to be more like Jesus.

DAY 2

THE VALUE OF ACCOUNTABILITY FRIENDSHIPS

When I saw that they were not really obeying the truth that is in the good news, I corrected Peter in front of everyone.

Galatians 2:14, *CEV*

Accountability friends keep you from getting off track and doing wrong things. Some things might seem right in your eyes, but according to Scripture, they are not right (see Proverbs 21:2). It's not about judging each other and getting mad at each other. It's about helping each other go toward the Lord—and going hand in hand.

In Galatians, you can see a very specific example of this kind of accountability:

> When Peter came to Antioch, I told him face-to-face that he was wrong. He used to eat with Gentile followers of the Lord, until James sent some Jewish followers. Peter was afraid of the Jews and soon stopped eating with Gentiles. He and the others hid their true feelings so well that even Barnabas was fooled. But when I saw that they were not really obeying the truth that is in the good news, I corrected Peter in front of everyone and said: "Peter, you are a Jew, but you live like a Gentile. So how can you force Gentiles to live like Jews?" (Galatians 2:11-14, *CEV*).

Basically, Paul got in Peter's face and said, "You're being a hypocrite. You're saying that you're not better than these guys, but then you eat only with the Jews and not everyone else." Paul faced him right in front of everybody.

That doesn't mean that if you are an accountability partner, you need to face your friend or embarrass him in front of everyone, but you need to be honest enough to speak the truth to him. As an accountability friend, you can't force someone to change, but you can definitely draw him to account.

Paul said, "Peter, this is not right. And if you think it is, I need you to give me an account. Explain to me why you are doing this if you think it is so right." If your friend can't give an account for his or her actions or attitude, your friend should be prepared to admit the wrong and commit to change.

Having accountability friends is very scriptural and godly. In fact, it helps you become more godly. It's important to remember, though, that these special friendships are not about judging each other. They're about loving each other enough to stay in each other's face.

Spend some more time praying throughout the day about one or two people you think you would like to invite into your life to keep you accountable.

List some of the advantages of an accountability friendship.

____

____

____

____

____

____

____

____

YOUR ACCOUNTABILITY FRIENDS MUST BE ON FIRE FOR GOD

Do not be unequally yoked together with unbelievers.

2 Corinthians 6:14

You can strike up an accountability friendship only with people who love God with all their heart and who are going to hold you to the same thing. If you've been hanging around people who aren't saved, who don't love God with all their heart or who are lukewarm, you may have to change friends. You may have to tell some or all of your current friends that you can't hang out with them anymore.

Some people say we need to witness to these people—we need to share the Lord with them—but you can't be out on a limb all by yourself trying to get them saved, hoping they'll get saved only so that you'll have Christian friends. You've got to get locked in with people who are accountable to get in your face and push you toward the Lord.

If you try to witness to your unsaved friends by yourself and hang out with them all the time, you will just get weaker and weaker. They end up picking you off instead of your drawing them into the kingdom of God.

The Bible says we are not to be "yoked together" with non-Christians. In other words, don't hang out with them too much, don't be committed to them, don't let their ideas infiltrate your mind, and don't let them influence you.

Hang out with people who love God. They should be your closest friends. Join a pack of on-fire, blazing followers of Christ who will stay in your face about going for God with all of your heart. Then you can go out together (maybe at school where there aren't many Christians around) and minister with strength to other people.

When your deep friendships are with people who really love God and are going after Him with all of their heart, you don't have to depend on yourself alone to stay strong. You can draw strength from other people. You may go out all alone, but you go back to your pack of wild friends and tell them what's going on and how you're ministering. You witness to people of the world, but you don't draw them in and let them be your closest friends.

The Bible is very clear about the relationships Christians should have with unbelievers. It's not just an issue of whether you should or shouldn't hang out with them. The Bible even asks you to examine what you really have in common with them: "For what fellowship has righteousness with lawlessness? And what communion has light with darkness? And what accord has Christ with Belial? Or what part has a believer with an unbeliever?" (2 Corinthians 6:14-15).

How could you possibly think unbelievers could be your best friends when what's deepest in your heart is completely different from what's in their heart?

Think about 2 Corinthians 6:14 today. Chew on it all day long. Memorize it, meditate on it, and think about any friendships you may need to cut off.

Have you gotten so close to some unbelievers that they've almost (or already) influenced you? Who are these questionable people? What unhealthy friendships do you need to cut off?

Keep praying for the accountability friends that God is going to bring your way. He's going to use your accountability friendships to change your life.

PAUL'S ACCOUNTABILITY FRIENDSHIPS

As iron sharpens iron, so a man sharpens the countenance of his friend.

Proverbs 27:17

This accountability friendship idea is not just a casual suggestion; it is an absolute imperative. The devil has used this area for a long time to pick people off. Most people don't want to be honest with others. They want to cover everything up and pretend everything is all right. They want to do everything alone. Then they wonder why they've backslid and they feel so far away from God.

I'm not simply presenting this as a good suggestion that you'll follow only if it just happens without much effort on your part. Finding an accountability friend is absolute survival mode—you've got to do it if you're going to keep your fire. Let's look at the example of Paul.

Paul went all over, traveling from village to village and town to town, starting churches and ministering like crazy. He was an awesome, blazing man of God, but he never went by himself. He always had someone around him like Barnabas, Silas or Timothy. Each man was in the other's face, pushing the other to go for God.

Now if anybody could stay strong and tight with God by himself, Paul should have been able to. However, Paul didn't trust himself to go it alone. He knew that out there was an evil world with way too many temptations to think that anyone could go it alone.

Yes, you have the power of God and the Word of God living inside of you, but we all need outward motivation to keep our hearts and our minds focused. Paul took other people with him to help keep his heart and his mind focused.

It's funny how much less temptation you're drawn into when other people are around. You would never even think about certain sins with other people around you.

Take some time today and meditate on these friendship Scriptures we've been talking about the past few days.

List two or three people who you think could be accountability friends like Paul had in Barnabas, Silas and Timothy.

Begin to pray that God will put the same thing on their heart and see if God makes a divine connection just like He did for Paul.

DAY 5

IN-YOUR-FACE FRIENDSHIPS

You can trust a friend who corrects you.

Proverbs 27:6, *CEV*

Accountability friendship is about friends being willing to get in each other's face. This is not the same as saying to someone, "Well, I'll pray for you, brother." Some of your Christian friends may be involved in the Christian cliché where they act like everything is all right, but inside they're not at all. They spend so much time playing sports or video games or doing other activities that they don't even feel close to anybody. There are people they say they're close to, but it's just because they go to the same youth group and sing "Kumbaya" and have goose bumps together. But they don't really know each other. Accountability friendships are different.

Accountability friendships say, "I'm going to get in your face, and I'm going to let you get in my face. If you see anything in my life that doesn't line up with the Word of God, I expect you to call me on it." I call them in-your-face friendships.

In these friendships, you give someone permission to hold you accountable—to ask you how your quiet time was, to find out what God spoke to you and to learn what's going on in your life. If you answer, "Well, nothing really," then your accountability friend gets in your face and says, "Wait just a minute! Aren't you growing in the Lord? Don't you want to change the world?" Your accountability partner gets in your face and says, "Listen, I will not stand for this. I love you too much to let you halfheartedly go through your quiet times and coast through your life. Let's pray about this."

Think back about the times somebody has gotten in your face and kept you from making a big mistake. That is what accountability friendships are about. These are people you allow to get in your face—not because they have to, but because you want them to. They help keep you from making big mistakes.

Write down a few areas you wish someone would get in your face about.

One sign of real maturity is allowing one of your parents to be an accountability partner. Basically, you tell you mom and dad (or just choose one) that you want to give them permission to get in your face whenever they think they need to. They may get in your face anyway, but you're giving them permission to get in your face about anything they see in you that doesn't look like something in Jesus' life.

What would your parents do if you said that to them? They would probably fall over and faint for about a month. It is a true sign of maturity when you want your mom and dad to push you to grow in the things of the Lord.

Keep praying over those people you listed yesterday who God might want to use in your life to be an accountability friend to you.

WHAT TO TALK ABOUT WITH AN ACCOUNTABILITY FRIEND

No longer do I call you servants, for a servant does not know what his master is doing; but I have called you friends, for all things that I heard from My Father I have made known to you.

John 15:15

This is Jesus' definition of *friendship*: "Things that I heard My Father speak in private I've made known to you." In other words, "I've told you about what My Father told Me. I've told you the deepest things in My heart that I wouldn't tell anyone else about. Now you're qualified to be My friend."

These accountability friendships you're developing should be with people with whom you are committed to sharing your heart, the very deepest part of yourself. Two or three people should really know everything about you—your deepest fears, desires and longings. These are not people with whom you should ever allow yourself to be fake. Jesus said, "In order for you to be qualified to be My friends, you have to hear the deepest things of My life."

If you want people to really pray for you, you've got to tell them the most important prayer matters in your life. Don't just ask them to pray for you on the surface: "Pray for me because I have a test in school this week." Start sharing your very gut with them, and let them seriously pray for you about things that really matter—a friendship at school, your parents, not feeling secure about yourself, or whatever you are going through that is really affecting who you are: "Please pray for my family. My dad got laid off, and I'm kind of worried about what's going to happen."

When you do that, you allow someone the privilege of coming into your life. Then that person can be a true friend to you because he or she knows what is going on and can really care about you.

Accountability friendships allow you to develop the kind of connections that can end up changing the world, the kind of relationships in which you connect heart to heart and soul to soul. You guys are actually hooked together. It's not some surface "Christian" friendship; you are people who really care about each other. You are family—the family of God. These are your brothers and sisters. You share your hearts on an ongoing basis and hold each other accountable to keep pressing toward the Lord.

Take some time and list some things here that you've wanted to share with other people, but you've never found someone who cared enough to really listen.

____

____

____

____

____

____

____

There is going to be a time when God will give you some friends with whom you can really share deep things from your heart. Keep asking. He has promised to hear you and answer.

DAY 7

COMMIT TO ACCOUNTABILITY FRIENDSHIPS

A man who has friends must himself be friendly, but there is a friend who sticks closer than a brother.

Proverbs 18:24

If you want to have friends, you have to be friendly.

How do you find an accountability friendship? You don't find such friendships by staying in a corner somewhere and hoping that God will bring someone to you. God will bring someone into your life but you have to show that you're interested.

You've got to show that you want to be this kind of friend to somebody else. You're not just looking for somebody to wait on you and listen to you. You've got to be willing to wait on, listen to and serve another person. You've got to show that you're interested in somebody else's life if you want somebody else to be interested in your life and help push you toward the Lord. You need to be like a heat-seeking missile going after the right kind of friend; your pursuit has to be relentless. Don't settle for whatever people are in your path at school or in your youth group.

Think about the kind of person you want for an accountability partner. This person should be somebody you look up to, someone you admire. You should see stuff in this person's life that looks like Jesus, and you should want in your life what this person has.

Look for somebody you want to be around, because you know that that person's character will rub off on you. Find someone with wisdom to speak into your life.

It doesn't have to be an older person, just someone you admire because you see God in his or her life. Since your friendship will be incredibly deep and you will share some very personal secrets, this person should be the same sex as you.

Continue to pray for your new friend now, and ask God to begin to mold that person's heart and draw that person toward you as an accountability friend. Begin to be friendly now and show yourself friendly to him or her.

Don't dump this heavy accountability thing on a person right away, though. Talk to the person about what is going on in his or her heart and see what you can pray together about. Later, you two can talk about being accountable to one another. Say something like, "Listen, I want you to get in my face about stuff. Maybe we could get in each other's faces and really push each other toward the Lord."

Now is your chance to go for it. Don't just sit there thinking about it anymore. Don't wait for someone to come up to you and ask you to be their accountability partner. You're going to have to go after it. It's not an option. It's not just a good idea. It's something you're going to have to relentlessly pursue.

Whatever your age—13, 14, 16, whatever—you're not too young to have an accountability partner who stays in your face. Somebody who is going to change the world has got to be hooked in with other people. Your closest friends should be people who are blazing maniacs and who want to change the world just like you do.

Now go out and begin to talk to the people you've been praying about. Talk to them and pursue accountability friendships in a very specific way. Decide right now what you plan to do in this accountability friendship. God bless you. You can change the world!

As a follower of Christ, I commit to surrounding myself with at least one or two accountable friends who will help push me toward the Lord. I will stay connected with my accountable friends all through my teen years. They can stay in my face, and I will stay in their faces so that by the time I am 20, I will have developed solid friendships that have pushed me to become all I can be as a follower of Christ.

______________________________ _______________

Your Signature Date

WEEK 7

LIVING A LIFESTYLE OF HOLINESS

DAY 1

BECOME A LIVING SACRIFICE

Therefore, I urge you, brothers, in view of God's mercy, to offer your bodies as living sacrifices, holy and pleasing to God—this is your spiritual act of worship.

Romans 12:1, *NIV*

Through Paul's words in Romans 12:1, the Bible encourages, exhorts and commands us to present our bodies as living sacrifices so that what we do will be an acceptable means of worship to God. In other words, we can worship with our lips, but God wants us to worship with our very lives.

The way you live should be an expression of worship to the Lord. He wants you to be holy, pure and acceptable to Him. Instead of offering your body to the world, offer it as a living sacrifice to God.

> Do not offer the parts of your body to sin, as instruments of wickedness, but rather offer yourselves to God, as those who have been brought from death to life; and offer the parts of your body to him as instruments of righteousness (Romans 6:13, *NIV*).

God wants you to have a holy lifestyle—to live in such a way that when people look at you, they say, "Wow! You look just like Jesus, like nothing I've ever seen before."

The Bible urges you to make sure that how you live lines up with what you say that you believe. Make sure that your words are not just a bunch of hot air coming out of your lips but that they are coming out of your life. The things you do and say should reflect what you believe. What you say you believe should be evident in the way you live.

James 2:18 says, "Show me your faith without your works, and I will show you my faith by my works." In other words, "You can see that I have faith because the way that I am living reflects that what I believe has really taken hold of my life."

As a follower of Christ, you have to refuse to let the worldly habits you see around you dominate your life. Although you have to live in this world, you don't have to be like the world. You can see through the games that the world plays, and you are smarter than that; you can live above it. You are called to live a lifestyle of worship that refuses to allow any habits from the world to creep into your life.

To sacrifice something is to completely give it away. In the Old Testament, when the priests sacrificed a lamb, they would actually kill it and present it to the Lord. Compare this to offering yourself as a living sacrifice. Although you don't actually die, you completely and totally give yourself over to the Lord. You present yourself to Him, saying, "Lord, use me. Use my life while I've still got breath in me to show this world what You really look like."

Take some time to meditate on Romans 12:1.

Write down a few ideas about what you can do to present yourself as a living sacrifice and to fully give yourself over to the Lord today.

Now go out and begin doing these things today.

LIVE FOR THE GLORY OF GOD

Whatever you do in word or deed, do all in the name of the Lord Jesus, giving thanks to God the Father through Him.

Colossians 3:17

God is concerned about all the things we do, even about our eating and drinking (see 1 Corinthians 10:31). We need to do everything in the name of the Lord; everything we do should give Him glory. He looks at our lives as through a microscope, and He wants to be glorified in everything we do and everything we say.

You can't allow yourself to think that the only time God sees your life is when you're at church or at youth group. You can't think that God looks only at certain parts of your life and not all of it. He wants every bit of your life to give Him glory. He wants you to be like a mirror. When people look at you, they should see a reflection of what He looks like.

You have to love God more than you love your old sinful habits. You have to love God more than you love secular music, cars, clothes or friends. You need to be drawn to God rather than to the world.

If you are determined that the things you do should be as worship to Him, then you need to stay in His presence all day long. Psalm 22:3 says that God inhabits the praises of His people. That means when you really praise and worship God, He hangs out with you all day long.

When you purpose in your heart to live holy and pure before Him, you can begin to stay in His presence all day long. The moment you think a sinful thought, you can sense things start to go wrong all around you. God can't hang out where there is sin.

The most awesome thing about the Christian life is that as you stay holy and pure, God's presence is available to you! He'll open up the door of your heart and cause things to happen to benefit you and put your life back together.

As a follower of Christ, you need to make a decision that whatever you do, you are going to bring God glory. You want people to look at your life and realize how awesome God is because of what they see.

Write out a couple of things that you have done in your life that portray Jesus well.

Now write out a couple of things you need to change today in order to portray Jesus in your life and bring Him greater glory.

AVOID VILE THINGS

I will set before my eyes no vile thing. The deeds of faithless men I hate; they will not cling to me.

Psalm 101:3, *NIV*

Something is wicked or vile when it is so offensive to the senses that you can't even stand it. It's repulsive. David says here, "I'm not going to put anything in front of my face that looks disgusting." It was a decision he made to stay in a worshipful lifestyle. He refused to set in front of himself anything that was vile to God.

This is the commitment of a follower of Christ: "I refuse to even accidentally allow any vile, disgusting thing in my life." This includes pornography, drugs, drinking, immorality, perversion, and sexual innuendos and content on TV, the Internet, in movies and in magazines—anything that leads to a sinful lifestyle or a sinful way of thinking. Make a decision today to set no vile thing before your eyes. Make a commitment not to pay attention to it. Turn your head when it tries to get your attention.

Take this verse from Psalm 101, memorize it and meditate on it all day long. Go for it with all your heart, and win this area of your life today.

Take a moment and list some vile or evil things that are easy to be exposed to, whether at school or at work, during the usual course of your day. What can you do to avoid those vile things?

MAKE A RADICAL COMMITMENT

"Everything is permissible"—but not everything is beneficial. "Everything is permissible"—but not everything is constructive.

1 Corinthians 10:23, *NIV*

When you commit your heart and life to Christ, there are a lot of things you could do but not everything will be in your best interest. As a young man or woman of God who is determined to be a true follower of Christ, you've got to decide what things you will refuse to let be a part of your life because they're not beneficial.

Just by going through this devotional book, you are expressing a desire to change the world, live for God, and be a ballistic Christian. Now is the time to choose to do the things you know will help you get where you want to go. There are things you could do that are not totally sin, but they're not going to take you where you want to go. You would end up on a treadmill going nowhere fast.

A lot of people say you can watch certain movies and just ignore all the bad parts or it's all right to listen to some music because the language isn't really that bad. However, as a Christian who wants to change the world, you need to say, "Yeah, I probably could do that, but there is some stuff I don't want inside me because it's not beneficial and it's not going to help me grow or change the world. I'm not a Christian who just wants to make it to heaven. I want to put my foot down and change my school and change the world, and I've got to start right now. I could get away with some of these things and still be a Christian and go to heaven, but that's not good enough for me. I want to change the world on my way to heaven."

> You, my brothers, were called to be free. But do not use your freedom to indulge in the sinful nature; rather, serve one another in love (Galatians 5:13, *NIV*).

Just because you're free, don't use your freedom to get caught up in the sinful nature. Before you know it, you are once again a slave to sin, the very thing from which Jesus has redeemed you.

You may need to make some radical commitments. For example, you may want to choose not to see R-rated movies or not to listen to secular music. Make these commitments with your whole heart. Don't long for things of the world.

Take a few minutes to pray and think about the things that would be permissible but not beneficial for you to do. Write out some specific things.

Now make a decision that even though you are permitted to do these things, you will refuse to do them because you are going to be a Christian who is set aside by God to really make a difference and change the world.

DAY 5

GET RID OF IDOLS

We know that an idol is nothing in the world, and that there is no other God but one.

1 Corinthians 8:4

If you're going to be a person who will change this world, you can't have any idols in your life. What is an idol? An idol is anything you love more than you love God. Your idol could be a person, or it could be an object. You don't usually intend to make somebody or something an idol. You just begin liking it more and more, and pretty soon you love it more than you love God. You can tell what obsesses you by how much time you spend with the object of your affections, how much you think about it and what you are willing to do for it. If you want to live a lifestyle of worship, you need to purpose in your heart to worship only God.

There is only one proper thing to do with an idol in your life, and this process is described in Exodus 32:20. The story is about the golden calf that the Israelites built. Everyone was worshiping and bowing down to this false god when Moses came off the mountain. Read Exodus 32:19-20. Now, consider the idols in your life. Try to think of what they have ever really done for you. You may think that they have done a lot, just like the Israelites thought their cow had delivered them from Egypt.

This Scripture describes exactly what Moses did with that idol. "Then [Moses] took the calf which they had made, burned it in the fire, and ground it to powder; and he scattered it on the water and made the children of Israel drink it" (Exodus 32:20).

Now that's drastic action. He said, "We're going to obliterate this idol so that you will never have the chance to worship this vile thing again." That is exactly what you and I need to do when we find idols creeping into our lives. We need to absolutely destroy them. In your life, this could mean throwing away secular music and/or getting rid of materialistic thinking. It could mean ending a relationship you have begun to value more than your relationship with God or that is causing compromise in your life.

You need to get rid of all idols so that there is no way you could ever worship them again. I know that this sounds like pretty drastic action, but it is so freeing when you absolutely rip the idols out of your life. I've seen thousands of teenagers make commitments to get rid of the secular music that most teenagers listen to. They've sent letters and pictures of themselves destroying their music and describing how free they finally are in Christ. They talk about having had chains around their necks and trying to live for God but always falling away. When they made a decision to crush their idols, they had great freedom and finally were able to start blazing for God like they wanted to.

I want you to list a few idols in your life that you need to obliterate.

Make a commitment today to do as Moses did with the calf and rip these vile things out of your life. Trash them today and see how much freedom God will give you in exchange.

RECOGNIZE THE VALUE OF A WORSHIPFUL LIFESTYLE

Create in me a pure heart, O God, and renew a steadfast spirit within me. Do not cast me from your presence or take your Holy Spirit from me. Restore to me the joy of your salvation and grant me a willing spirit, to sustain me.

Psalm 51:10-12, *NIV*

Why is it so important to have a worshipful lifestyle? Basically, worshiping God is bowing down before His throne and acknowledging His awesomeness. The only way He allows you to come before His throne is after all the junk from your life has been removed. You don't have to be perfect; you just have to be humble and admit to the Lord where you've blown it and then do everything possible to rid your life of idols and be clean. Quote Scripture, rip the bad stuff out of your life, and live completely holy before Him.

The most awesome thing you can know is that your life is completely right and holy. When you have a clear conscience before God, He blows your face off, and His presence comes down and hovers over you all day and all night. You are living your life before the throne of God. You're into God and He's into you; you're speaking to Him and He's speaking to you.

As you come into His presence, check your heart and make sure nothing is standing between you and God:

> Therefore, if you bring your gift to the altar, and there remember that your brother has something against you, leave your gift there before the altar, and go your way. First be reconciled to your brother, and then come and offer your gift (Matthew 5:23-24).

Jesus talked about offering a gift of sacrifice to the Lord. When you have something in your heart against somebody, you should leave your gift, go, and make things right before you come back. You need to be completely clean when you come before the Lord in worship. If something is not right in your life or heart—whether it is between you and another person or between you and God—you've got to make things right so that you are as clean as possible.

If you want God to use you to change the world, you've got to make sure everything in your life is pure and holy so that He can walk with you all day long and you can feel His indescribable presence. If your conscience is bothering you, don't ignore it; take time to confess it to the Lord and let Him give you the courage to make it right.

Write down anything that might be standing in your way of an awesome time of worshiping God.

____

____

____

____

____

____

____

____

____

Commit to make things right, even if that means talking it through with someone before you worship, so that you can walk in holiness and purity before God today.

DAY 7

COMMIT TO A LIFESTYLE OF WORSHIP

Denying ungodliness and worldly lusts, we should live soberly, righteously, and godly.

Titus 2:12

We've been talking about your living a lifestyle of holiness with no vile thing in your life. That means living a life in which people look at you and see a reflection of Jesus: Everything you say and do is incredibly pure.

Practically speaking, what should you do about your lifestyle and the things in your life? Begin to look at all your habits. The way you talk, the way you act, the way you use your spare time, the way you think—these are all important. Now ask yourself how they compare to Scripture. How does the way you talk, act, think and spend your time compare to Scripture? How do those things compare to what Jesus or other people of the Bible thought was important? What does God have to say about these areas?

As a follower of Christ, you are going to have to say no to some things other people, maybe even other Christians, would say yes to. Your desire to change the world does not permit you to do things other Christians might get away with or feel like they could do. Your seriousness and focus demand a higher level of living and caliber of intensity. You don't do what comes naturally; you measure everything by the Word of God. You refuse to allow yourself to give in to the usual way of living because you have a higher standard and a higher calling. Your whole youth group might be doing something and everyone might be saying that it is okay, but that doesn't matter. You have made a radical commitment to blast every piece of vile activity out of your life, because you love God more than you love the world.

Today, I want you as a follower of Christ to make the commitment to demand holiness and purity of yourself. As soon as you detect sin in your life, be committed to getting it out and allowing no vile thing to stand before you.

As a follower of Christ, I commit to living a lifestyle of worship so that in everything I say and do, I give God glory. I commit to put no vile thing before my eyes. I refuse to allow into my life any influences of the world that would draw me away from God, no matter what the cost or what other people say. My commitment is to change the world. To do that, I've got to be absolutely pure in everything I say and do.

______________________________ _______________

Your Signature Date

WEEK 8

COURTSHIP OVER DATING

THE DATING GAME

The Lord will guide you always; he will satisfy your needs in a sun-scorched land and will strengthen your frame.

Isaiah 58:11, *NIV*

Take three minutes and memorize today's verse.

Followers of Christ can see through all the games the world throws at them, including all the games connected to the dating scene. The dating scene is designed to make you feel stupid or weird if you don't have a date. You're supposed to feel as if you have to have somebody to love or have on your shoulder or have your arm wrapped around in order to be worth anything. You're supposed to feel like a social misfit if you don't have someone to go out with.

The dating game is full of gimmicks, like going out with who looks the cutest or who makes you look the hottest. You become so busy trying to be what you think the other person wants you to be that you are never really yourself. And you don't know if the person really likes you or not, because you have been fake with each other the whole time.

It's a "cutesy, cutesy" game of wondering all the time what so-and-so is saying about so-and-so and which guy likes which girl and which girl likes which guy and who is saying such-and-such about so-and-so and who wants to date someone else but they're mad at each other because . . . you get the idea. It's just a big game that distracts you from what God really wants to do in you and through you.

This whole teenage dating thing totally rips people out of their walk with God. They get so distracted by some guy or girl who mesmerizes them that they totally forget they really should be seeking God and not another person.

I have talked to many young people who have compromised their Christian walk by allowing themselves to get into the situation described above. The Bible talks about loving the Lord your God with all of your heart, soul and mind (see Matthew 22:37). Your desire for Him needs to be stronger than your desire to date and stronger than your desire for the acceptance you think you might get from dating. You might think you need to have a boyfriend or girlfriend because you want to be loved by somebody. Let me tell you, God knows what you need. The problem is this: If you think you need somebody, you're not ready for anybody. Your need for love and acceptance cannot be met by another person; it can only be met by God.

Today's verse says that God will give you whatever you need. God knows what you need—He made you. He knows what you're made of, and He knows how to meet your needs. You don't need a boyfriend or girlfriend. You need a relationship with Jesus. You need to be tied up in God more than you have ever been in your entire life. The Bible says that He knows your needs. So if you feel as if you need another person, you really need to quote and chew on this verse all day long. Trust that God will do what He says because He never lies. He promised, "I will meet every one of your needs."

I know that not playing the dating game sounds drastic, but if you are going to change the world, then you are going to have to see through this game. It will only pull you down and suck the life out of you. You will soon forget the fire that you once had.

Have you played the dating game or are you playing it right now? How has it compromised your walk with God?

____

____

____

____

____

____

Take Philippians 4:19 and chew on it today, anytime you feel that you have a need. Concentrate on this Scripture, especially if you feel that you need a boyfriend or girlfriend. Then you'll have the confidence that God alone will supply all your needs.

COURTSHIP VERSUS DATING (PART 1)

The wisdom of the prudent is to give thought to their ways, but the folly of fools is deception.

Proverbs 14:8, *NIV*

Developing a courting relationship is completely different from developing a dating relationship. I want you to develop a level of maturity that allows you to see all of the games the world throws at you. To do that, the first thing you have to do is to back away from the whole dating game and commit to go after God with all your heart. Then find healthy ways to develop a friendship relationship with someone of the opposite sex. This friendship may or may not lead to a romantic relationship, but the friendship should be your first priority. Don't just jump from one relationship to another, depending solely on who's available at the time. That's a sickening game, and you have to be smarter than that.

Be confident that God will supply all your needs. Choose to back away from any kind of dating relationship and go full blast into God. Find out some courtship principles from the Scriptures. You will be able to use them to develop a wholesome relationship that will ultimately lead to marriage.

Look again at the Scripture verse for today. The point being made here is that if you're going to be wise, you need to give thought to your ways and thought to your steps. Don't be sucked into the dating game. You need to think about what you're doing before you do it. Just because everyone else is dating doesn't mean that you should. Just because everyone else kisses on their first date or everybody else gets into some kind of sexual activity by their third date doesn't mean that you should. You have to think about your ways.

Your ways are your actions. Your actions include the way you flirt, the way you wink or smile, the way you flip your hair for a guy or flex your muscles when you walk by a girl. Think about the things you do that attract or lure people because of your desire for attention. Remember, God will supply all your needs. You don't need a guy or a girl checking you out every time you walk by just to make you feel as if you're worth something. God says you're worth a lot because He made you. He says you're beautifully and wonderfully made (see Psalm 139:14). You're awesome! He put you together and made you an incredible young man or woman of God.

Think about what you do and why you do it. Give thought to your ways. If you love the Lord with all your heart, put no vile thing before your eyes. You don't want to look like the world anyway. When you think about what you do before you do it, it begins to change the way you do things. Don't just do what is done on some TV show and think that it's okay because everybody does it—it isn't okay and everyone isn't doing it. Followers of Christ, wise young men and women, are giving thought to their steps. Before you do something, before you ask somebody out, before you play the typical dating game, think about what you're thinking about doing. You shouldn't want to look like the world.

Take a few minutes and think about your ways and steps. What actions have you done or are doing to attract the attention of the opposite sex—in other words, what do you need to stop doing?

DAY 3

COURTSHIP VERSUS DATING (PART 2)

A simple man believes anything, but a prudent man gives thought to his steps.

Proverbs 14:15, *NIV*

In the chapter about accountability friendships, we discussed principles regarding how to proceed with a friendship. You can apply those directly to a courtship as well. In a courtship, you think through all the ramifications of the relationship. You're not pulled into anything since you're thinking about where the relationship is going. Ask yourself some serious questions: *Am I really pursuing God? Is this relationship going to help me become a better follower of Christ? Is this relationship distracting me from my relationship with God? Am I letting this person become an idol in my life?* If you honestly answer all of these questions in the right way, then you are giving thought to your steps.

What can you take from how to develop accountability friendships and apply to a courtship relationship? (Also keep in mind what you know about not letting vile thoughts or distractions get in your way to the Lord.)

The most important thing to remember is that courtship is about using godly principles to build a friendship that could lead to a romance and, ultimately, to marriage. Now *that* is different from the American dating scene.

Take a few moments and list here what you think the advantages are of courtship versus the typical dating game.

It is time to change the dating scene. Let it start with you today.

DAY 4

FRIENDSHIP BEFORE COURTSHIP

Flee also youthful lusts; but pursue righteousness, faith, love, peace with those who call on the Lord out of a pure heart.

2 Timothy 2:22

You must determine to have a friendship before a courtship relationship if you and the other person want to really get to know each other. It's amazing to me how people can sit by each other in a class, and a week later they are dating—and a week after that they are in a sexual relationship, but they really don't know each other. Some say that it's love at first sight, but I don't think they even know the definition of love. They figure that it's okay to go out and get involved if they are "in love."

The Bible says in Colossians 3:1-2, "Since, then, you have been raised with Christ, set your hearts on things above, where Christ is seated at the right hand of God. Set your minds on things above, not on earthly things" (*NIV*).

I want you to understand what that Scripture means. You should be in control of where your heart goes. You choose to set your heart on the things above and not on the things of the earth. I want to share something with you that you may find hard to believe: The whole concept of falling love is not in the Bible. "Falling in love" really is nothing more than infatuation. Some people try to make a distinction between being infatuated and falling in love, but there is no difference in the way we use the words in our society.

The dictionary definition of "infatuation" is "to make foolish, to deprive of sound judgment, to inspire with a foolish or shallow love or affection." In other words, someone who is infatuated looks like a fool because he or she is doing something without using sound judgment.

The very expression "falling in love" implies lack of control. "I don't know . . . it was the weirdest thing. I was just walking along, minding my own business, when all of a sudden I fell down. Then *boom!* There I was—in love!" The Bible says that we don't fall or trip into anything. We aren't pulled into anything beyond our will. Don't be like a big gaping satellite dish, wide open to any love signals that might fly your way. You're smarter than that. Keep a pure heart.

The trouble is that this concept of falling in love has been around for so long that even your parents sometimes encourage it. They'll say something like, "You're in love, aren't you?" So you think, *Well, I guess I am. Should I be? I don't know. Maybe I'm weird if I'm not.* Just because your parents use these words or are familiar with the concept doesn't mean that falling in love is holy and godly. Most young people do what they have seen other people do. We know that love is from God, so isn't falling in love from God, too? Wrong. Falling in love isn't love; it is infatuation.

The kind of love God has for you has nothing to do with falling. He doesn't want you falling into anything, because you'll just fall back out again. You aren't a feeble little thing who falls into a hole. That is not what God created you for. God created you as a man or woman with destiny, focus and purpose. He created you to take wise steps according to His wisdom; this, in turn, will lead you to a fulfilled and happy lifestyle. If you fall into anything, including love, you will not benefit in the long run.

It's time to think about what it means to set your heart on the thing above. If you set your heart and mind on things above, then you will not get tripped up into this falling-in-love thing, and you will make a decision to have wholesome friendships. Make sure you have been in a healthy friendship for at least a year before you consider romance.

True friendship takes time. Take the time to know what really makes this person tick. What's important to this person? What dreams and aspirations does this person have? Does this person really love God with his or her whole heart? Does the relationship between the two of you draw both of you closer to God or does it pull you away from Him? What does your accountability partner think? If you have godly parents, what do they think? These are questions you ask *before* you get into a serious relationship. They'll help you make a wise decision.

Take 2 Timothy 2:22 and chew on it all day. Concentrate on keeping your heart pure. Don't get lured into the things of this world.

Have you ever "fallen in love"? What does that expression mean to you? What kind of love does God want you to share with someone of the opposite sex?

DAY 5

FREE FROM IMMORALITY

Flee sexual immorality.

1 Corinthians 6:18

As you begin to walk down the road of having a holy courtship that reflects a pure relationship, recognize that the devil will try to mess you up physically. Even if you obey all the principles of having a friendship first and accountability in your life, the devil can still entice you into sexual immorality as you walk in your courtship.

Paul pointed out that you are to "flee sexual immorality." You are not to take part in sexual relations outside of marriage. Then Paul went on to say, "Every sin that a man does is outside the body, but he who commits sexual immorality sins against his own body. Or do you not know that your body is the temple of the Holy Spirit who is in you, whom you have from God, and you are not your own? For you were bought at a price; therefore glorify God in your body" (1 Corinthians 6:18-20).

Paul meant that when you commit a sexual sin, you harm yourself not just morally but also physically. Your body is the temple of the Holy Spirit. In other words, God lives inside of you. Don't take this thing that God lives inside of and use it for anything impure.

God is looking for a generation of young people who have decided that they are going to protect their hearts, their minds and their bodies. They are not just going to say no to intercourse. They are going to say no to any kind of sexual intimacy, including petting, oral sex—any sexual involvement whatsoever.

If you have already been involved with someone sexually, then make a commitment now to stay pure and never be sexually involved again until you're married. It's sort of like a second virginity. Once you get the revelation, the lights come on and you say, "I'm going to keep my body pure until the day I'm married." If you have never had sex, then great; never have it while you're unmarried.

There have been cases of young ladies getting pregnant even though they've never had sexual intercourse. What? How could that happen? They did not have intercourse, but they were fooling around enough that semen from the guy was able to get inside her and she got pregnant. That's why committing to not having the act of sex, or sexual intercourse, isn't enough. You must absolutely stay away from any situation where you even come close to intercourse.

Unfortunately, some people think that they are staying pure just because they do not have sexual intercourse. Fleeing from immorality is not about how close you can come without getting caught or pregnant. It is about living with a pure heart so that you do not fool around with any kind of sexual impropriety. It is about honoring the Word of God so much and respecting that other person so much that you would not dare lay a hand on him or her in a sexual way until you are married. The Bible says to treat the opposite sex like a brother or sister, with absolute purity (see 1 Timothy 5:1-2). A great way to live up to that high standard is to stay around accountability friends and to keep the lights on wherever you are. If the lights are on and friends are around, then it is hard to mess up.

God is looking for followers of Christ who are radically, passionately committed to every part of their lives being totally clean. This is the time to commit your body—every part of it—to purity. Until you find the one who is committed to be with you forever and you actually have the wedding ceremony in front of a preacher and a whole crowd, never allow anyone to touch you.

Please memorize 1 Corinthians 6:18. Chew, chew, chew on it all day long.

List some things you can do when tempted by immoral behavior.

____

____

____

____

____

____

DAY 6

GUARD YOUR HEART

Above all else, guard your heart, for it is the wellspring of life.

Proverbs 4:23, *NIV*

The whole idea of pursuing a courtship when God says it is right versus having a dating relationship with someone has to do with guarding your heart. Your heart is one of the most precious parts of your being. If you let just any person come into your heart and lure you into a relationship, then your heart is going to get busted up, ripped apart, broken up and stomped on.

I'm sure you've seen this happen all around you. Look at the people in your school and see how many are hurt because someone let them down, how many have had their emotions crushed, and how many girls have gotten pregnant. We're talking about not "falling in love" and just letting your lips fly onto anyone who comes your way. Letting a boy put his arm around you or a girl hang on your shoulder just because that person looks halfway cool or popular is *bogus*.

You have to guard your heart. You have to protect it from getting crushed and smashed. Out of your heart comes the wellspring of life. It is the very center of your life, your joy and zest for living. You're a follower of Christ, so you can't walk through life like most people do. Their hearts have been beaten up and stabbed, and walked on and stabbed, and walked on and walked on. One day you may want to get married. If you have given your heart to every person you ever went on a date with, what will make this person you want to marry so special?

You have to guard your heart. When you give it away, you give away the remote control for your life. Just like someone could take the remote control for a toy car and run the car off a cliff or smash it into a wall, some people do that when you give them your heart. They smash you up and then laugh when you crash.

Guard your heart. Out of it comes the wellspring of life. But out of it can also come misery if you let people walk on it and stab it. You have to guard it, protect it, and set it on things above. Then when God has the right relationship for you, you can pursue a courtship. Continue to guard your heart until you have enough trust in the friendship that you know and have confidence that your heart will not be abused or misused.

Take some time to meditate on Proverbs 4:23, and think about what you can do to guard your heart. Write out two or three ways.

DAY 7

COMMIT TO CHOOSING A COURTSHIP RELATIONSHIP

As He who called you is holy, you also be holy in all your conduct.

1 Peter 1:15

We've been talking about how a follower of Christ doesn't get involved in a falling-in-love kind of dating but rather uses sound judgment in deciding what to do. I want to give some guiding principles for your relationship so that when the time is right for you to develop a courtship, you go about it in a godly way. You don't want to have gone through your teen years having had a dozen, six or even a couple of dating relationships. I know Christians do that all over the place, but you have a different agenda. You want to change the world.

Don't just look for someone to slap your lips on. Don't just look for somebody to be the other half of a good-looking couple. Look at how you can change the world. If God brings the right person into your life, you can change the world together. Let's talk about some principles you can use to guide a courtship.

What are some areas in your personal development that you would like to grow in before you get into a courtship? In other words, maybe there are some areas in your life where you are immature. Are there areas where you have been struggling with sin? Maybe you have some thought habits you have been struggling with. Are there Scriptures you have wanted to memorize? We all have areas where we know we need to be stronger.

When you get into a real relationship, you don't want to give 25 or 50 percent of yourself. You don't want to be some slob Christian who is barely hanging out with God. You want to be the very best that you can be when you give yourself to another person. You want to be full, whole and developed in every area.

Think about the areas you want to develop before you would ever consider getting involved with a deep relationship. These areas could be bad habits you want to get rid of or sin you want to deal with. Maybe you want more maturity in the way you think and the way you talk.

List a few of the areas where you know you need to be stronger.

____

____

____

____

____

____

____

____

Now think about what you want to see developed in a guy or girl before you start a courtship with that person. You want to know that he or she has lived a consistent Christian life for at least a year or two before you date. You want to make sure the other person is not on the rebound from somebody else and only wants you because he or she wants to have somebody—anybody. Is this person submissive to his or her parents? Has this person made a commitment to be a follower of Christ and to read through the Bible? Does this person seek the Lord? A yes answer to the last two questions should be a prerequisite.

You don't want to date just anybody who takes a liking to you. When you have your heart and life together as a follower of Christ, a lot of people will find you attractive. You have to have high standards. Don't just consider if he is tall, dark and handsome. Set standards for what his character will be like. You don't want somebody who had been throwing her lips all over every guy in town and who is now sweet on you. The standards that you choose for a guy or girl should be different from what people in the world choose.

List five or six standards that you set for somebody you would enter into a courtship relationship with.

___

___

___

___

___

___

___

___

___

___

___

Once you have grown to the point that you are ready for and have met somebody you think is also ready for a courtship relationship, think about how to proceed. You need to set some guidelines now for what you want later (give thought to your ways). What do you want in your friendship with that person before you ever begin a courtship?

Consider having an accountability friendship with that person for at least a year. You should know each other and be friends for at least a year before you would think of giving your heart away. Make sure that both of you are reading through the Scriptures. Make sure that both of you are committed to change the world. Commit together that both of you will run from sexual immorality.

What do you want to do in your relationship to protect your fire and purity before God? Determine together to read the Bible or worship together for a specific amount of time each week. Don't lose your focus. Stay consumed with God, not with each other. Don't go on dates every single night or even every weekend. Don't spend hours on the phone every day. Stay balanced. Keep your other friendships—those you had before you met as well as new ones you'll develop together.

List several ways you will proceed to be pure and holy in your courtship relationship.

____

____

____

____

____

____

____

____

____

As a follower of Christ, I commit to establish a courtship relationship and to avoid the typical dating relationship in whatever kind of romance I pursue. Because my body is the temple of the Holy Spirit, I commit to keep my body pure from sexual intercourse and any other kind of physical contact that would promote sexual indiscretion. I commit to live by a higher standard than the world's, to keep my heart pure and to not play the dating game.

______________________________ ______________

Your Signature Date

WEEK 9

HONORING YOUR PARENTS

DAY 1

HOW TO BE BLESSED

Children, obey your parents in the Lord, for this is right. "Honor your father and mother,"which is the first commandment with a promise: "that it may be well with you and you may live long on the earth."

Ephesians 6:1-3

Young people who have had anything to do with the Lord have heard this Scripture passage a thousand times, usually out of their parent's mouth. These are the verses that most young people wish weren't even in the Bible, because their parents use this passage against them so much. However, if you're going to be a follower of Christ, you have to be committed to living this Scripture, even when you don't feel like it and even when it doesn't make sense to you. You have to be committed to honoring your mom and dad. The Bible says that if you honor them, you will live well and long and you will be blessed. If you honor them, God will put His anointing on everything you do, and it will all turn to gold and be successful.

Some people wonder, *Why is everything going wrong in my life? Why does everything seem to be falling down around me? Why does it seem like God's blessing is not on my life as it seems to be for other people?* If things aren't going well for you, you need to see if the blessing of God has been taken from your life.

First of all, have you given your life to the Lord? Are you living free from sin? Are you going after God and reading the Word with all your heart? Now, check if you are honoring your parents. God gives His word that if you honor your mother and father, things will go well with you.

A lot of people think that the more they can get away with, the better their life will be. They think, *If I can just do this behind my parents' back and not get caught, then I'll have more fun*. The

Bible says that just the opposite is true: It's only when you honor your parents that things go well for you. That's when your life is pulled back together. That's when God's blessing and anointing come on your life.

It doesn't matter what other people seem to be getting away with. It's not important that other kids are sneaking around without their parents knowing about it. One day, people will wonder about you: Why do you have a car, though you're only 16? Why do your parents allow you to go overseas on mission trips? Why do your parents allow you to do a lot of really cool things? It is simply because God's blessing is on your life and your parents trust you because you've proven to be worthy. You will have a much happier life with more fulfillment and will be able to do more things than if you had played the world's game.

Memorize Ephesians 6:1-3 today. Think about what you can do today to honor your mother and father.

List four or five things you will do this week to show your parents that you honor them.

____

____

____

____

____

____

____

____

DAY 2

HONOR EVEN WHEN IT'S HARD

Honor all people.

1 Peter 2:17

Many people are confused about the difference between honoring and obeying. As children, we need to obey our parents. However, as we grow older, we can make a decision about whether or not to honor our parents. Some people may find it difficult to honor their mom and dad because of some things their parents have done or said that have not been very godly.

Maybe your parents aren't saved. You might be thinking, *How can I honor my mom and dad if they don't even love the Lord?* When you honor others, you respect them because of the position they hold. You don't necessarily honor them because they deserve it or because of anything they have done. You honor them because their position is worthy of honor. And don't forget that they, like you, were made in God's likeness, so when you honor them, you also honor God.

Presidents of countries all over the world travel with grand entourages. Parades are held in their honor, people salute them, crowds cheer them, and other countries roll out the red carpet for them. Wherever they go, they are shown great respect. Some of them may be terrible leaders. They may have policies that don't make sense. They may dress funny. They may be really boring speakers. However, because they lead a country, people show them honor.

It is the same way with your parents. They may do things you don't like. They may have rules for your house that you don't agree with. You may not like their clothes or the way they do their hair. You may not like the food they fix or their hobbies. They may have habits that irritate you. All of that aside, God has given them specific positions as your parents.

Of all the people in the world, God chose these two to bring you into the world. He could have used anybody, but He chose these two. Why? Who knows why? It was God's decision, and He gave them the positions of being your biological parents. They are, by virtue of their positions, worthy of receiving your honor. So whether or not you like what they do, whether or not you like their rules and regulations, God says that He will bless you if you honor them.

If you're not already doing so, right now is the time to begin to honor you mom and dad, no matter what they've done or said. It's time to begin to esteem them because of the position God gave them and because it honors God. Remember that showing respect is not based on whether you feel like it; it's a decision you make. You have to say, "I know God gave my parents their positions, and I'm going to make a decision to honor them, no matter how I feel and no matter what they've done. I will honor them because they are my mom and dad."

Is there anything you do or don't do that dishonors your parents? Anything that shows disrespect? What do you need to change so that you honor your parents?

DAY 3

REBELLION EQUALS WITCHCRAFT

For rebellion is as the sin of witchcraft, and stubbornness is as iniquity and idolatry.

1 Samuel 15:23

Take five minutes and memorize this verse.

The Bible says rebellion is just like the sin of witchcraft. Most of us would agree that we would never want to become involved with witchcraft because we don't want to deal with demons. Most of us don't want to fool around with the occult. But the Bible says that rebellion is the same as witchcraft. Of course, we know that God looks at sins equally: Murdering someone and lying to someone are both sins. However, rebellion has an added twist to it.

God is very serious about the authorities that He sets up in our lives. He wants us to obey and honor them. He has given your parents authority in your life. He knows that when you buck the authority system that He has set up in your life—when you rip it up and disrespect it—you are disrespecting what God has put in your life to help you develop into a responsible young man or woman for Him. He has put these guidelines and people in your life to protect you. When you go against them, you get out of the protection of God. In other words, when you rebel against your parents, you make yourself open game for the devil. When you disrespect and dishonor your parents, you make yourself a target for Satan.

Rebellion seems to be at an all-time high in terms of popularity. Young people brag about how they sneak around on their parents—how they got to do things and their parents never found out. Other people show rebellion by calling their parents by their first names, using a certain tone of voice with their parents or manipulating their parents (that is, playing Mom against Dad, or vice versa—especially if the parents don't live together). These may be typical things to do in the world, and you might feel as if you have to compete with them if you're going to have any fun; but they're all signs of rebellion. They're all acts of disrespect and dishonor.

When you begin to toy with this command, you get out of God's protection and become an open target for the devil. It's just like witchcraft. You might as well go ahead and do witchcraft because that's how bad it is. God's protection plan is better than any insurance plan. You're in perfect hands with God when you do what He desires for you to do as a young man or woman of God.

As a follower of Christ, you would agree, I'm sure, that you would never want to touch witchcraft. You need to have that same kind of conviction and fervency about the way you treat your parents. You never want to be in any kind of rebellion, even if it's only in your attitude. For example, there are going to be times when your parents ask you to do things you don't want to do. You have to decide if you are going to walk in rebellion or if you are going to walk in submission.

For the rest of your life, you will need to submit to somebody. You will need to submit to your boss. The Bible tells husbands and wives to submit to each other. Wherever you live, you will need to submit to the government. It won't always be easy to submit. You have to make a decision: *If God has put these authorities in my life, then I am going to comply with the things that they are going to ask of me.*

As a follower of Christ, you have to be absolutely committed to want no part of any kind of rebellion in your life. Be radically submissive to your parents and pleasing to the Lord. Pray this prayer right now:

> *Father, I recognize that rebellion is the same as witch craft in Your eyes. Right now I choose to completely walk way from all rebellion against my authorities, especially my parents. Forgive me for my rebellious ways and attitudes. From now on I choose to submit to You by submitting to them and honoring them as the authorities that You've put in my life to protect me. In Jesus' name, amen.*

DAY 4

HAVE AN ATTITUDE OF HONOR

Your attitude should be the same as that of Christ Jesus.

Philippians 2:5, *NIV*

Take some time to memorize Philippians 2:5 right now. Study it until you can say it five times without looking.

When we talk about honoring parents, attitude is a major area that we need to examine. Write down what you think having the same attitude as that of Jesus Christ means. What kind of attitude did He have?

____
____
____
____
____
____
____
____

Many times you might think to yourself, *Well, I'll be obedient to my mom and dad, but I won't be happy about it.* You have to ask yourself if you're really honoring them when you obey with a bad attitude. For example, your mom tells you to take out the garbage, but you're watching TV. She says it again and again. Finally, you get up, stomp out of the room, take out the garbage, sigh real heavily and mumble stuff under your breath, and stomp back in—making sure everyone knows that you're really mad. Did you obey your mother? Yes. Did you honor her? No! Sure, you obeyed—after being asked several times—but you didn't honor her. It's not enough just to do the thing. You have to do it with an honorable attitude and a submissive, joyful spirit. God will bless you for having the right attitude.

Your attitude makes all the difference. It's your choice about the kind of attitude you have. As a follower of Christ, you're not manipulated by your circumstance. You don't think, *I don't feel like doing this, so I'm going to get mad and stomp my feet.* You're bigger than that. You have the God of the universe living inside of you. You want to live for Him with all your heart. You want to change the world and do incredible things in your school and all over the place. You can choose to have the same attitude as that of Christ Jesus: a humble, submissive heart toward your mom and dad, bending over backward to do whatever they want you to do.

The attitude of the world may have infected you so much that you don't even realize that when you stomp your feet, you're displaying the attitude of the world. Many times you may say things about your parents behind their back. Well, it's time for you as a follower of Christ to stand up and be counted as someone who loves your parents and honors them. You honor them by making them look good in front of other people. You honor them when you don't let them look bad.

I want to encourage you to have an attitude that would absolutely blow your mom and dad away. Develop an attitude that causes other people (both teenagers and adults) to be blown away because they see in the way you treat your mom and dad the same attitude as Jesus.

Let me give you some specific tips on how to change your attitude. When your mom and dad talk to you, don't say things under your breath. Look them right in the eye and answer them with honor, dignity and respect. Answer them with a "Yes, sir," or "Yes, ma'am." These expressions may be more common in the South, but that doesn't matter. You need to start honoring your parents when you talk to them. Let your respect be reflected in your language.

Another specific thing to give attention to is your tone of voice. Don't be sarcastic, and never raise your voice to your parents. Hold your tongue. Think before you speak. Never, ever say anything out of anger or disrespect, and don't mutter under your breath as you walk away.

Something else to avoid is talking about your parents behind their back. Don't talk about them when they're not around, and never run your parents down, making them look bad. Your own mouth will make you look bad in the end. If you have a problem with your mom and dad, talk confidentially to your pastor or youth pastor. Even if your parents aren't saved, your pastor or youth pastor can help you come up with a workable solution to your problem. Show this world that you're a Christian with an honorable attitude toward your parents.

Write down some things that you can do today that would change your attitude in areas where you have had a bad attitude. Commit to do these things today.

OBEY WITH YOUR WHOLE HEART

Serve wholeheartedly, as if you were serving the Lord, not men.

Ephesians 6:7, *NIV*

Today's verse is actually from a passage that describes how slaves should obey their earthly masters:

> Slaves, obey your earthly masters with respect and fear, and with sincerity of heart, just as you would obey Christ. Obey them not only to win their favor when their eye is on you, but like slaves of Christ, doing the will of God from your heart. Serve wholeheartedly, as if you were serving the Lord, not men, because you know that the Lord will reward everyone for whatever good he does, whether he is a slave or free (Ephesians 6:5-8, *NIV*).

Although you might feel like a slave to your mom and dad, I'm not implying that you are a slave. The point is this: God is giving you some guidelines for how you should respond to authority in your life: Obey the authorities in your life the same way you obey God—wholeheartedly. That's the kind of attitude you want to have toward your parents. Whether they're looking or not, you're going to go by their wishes because that honors them.

You want to bend over backward to do whatever you possibly can to honor your parents. Don't just go by the letter of the law; go by the spirit of the law. Don't come in two minutes after curfew and argue about whether or not you were late; come in half an hour early! Go crazy to show them that you're not trying to get away with anything, but you want to have a servant, submissive heart. What you're really doing is pleasing the Lord. God is pleased with a heart that is submissive, not one just barely trying to get by with the letter of the law.

You want to do more than what your parents expect from you. If they ask you to wash the dishes, sweep and mop the kitchen floor as well. If they ask you to make your bed, clean your whole room. (I know it could take years to get your whole room clean, but next time it should go faster.) Show them from your heart that you're not just doing barely enough to get by. Do more than they ask of you. Go overboard because you want to be sure that they understand beyond a shadow of a doubt that you are someone who has a submissive attitude toward them and you're honoring them in what you do.

List three or four areas where you could go overboard to really show your mom and dad that you're not just doing what they say, you're doing what they wish, what they really want.

Your perspective toward your parents should be, "Your wish is my command. I want to do even more than you ask, and I'll be happy doing it. I know that by doing that, I'll be pleasing to the Lord." Meditate on Ephesians 6:7, and think about what it really means to serve your parents wholeheartedly.

WAYS TO HONOR YOUR PARENTS

Cease listening to instruction, my son, and you will stray from the words of knowledge.

Proverbs 19:27

We are talking this week about honoring your parents. I want to talk about some specific ways you can honor your parents.

First of all, you can honor your parents by listening to them. The Bible says, "He who answers a matter before he hears it, it is folly and shame to him" (Proverbs 18:13). Most young people don't want to listen to what their parents have to say. They're tapping their feet or sighing loudly or watching TV. Whatever the method, they're not really tuned in and listening to their parents.

It's time to stop everything, chill out, and listen to what Mom and Dad are saying. Maybe they're giving you some advice. Maybe they're telling you something that's really going to protect you and keep you from messing up your life. Maybe it will help you get through college. Maybe it's a tip that will help you in a relationship or a friendship. Even if what you hear sounds boring or doesn't immediately make sense to you, the Bible says that if you're going to be respectful, you really need to listen.

List some things that you can do or stop doing that will help you really listen when your mom and dad are talking (for example, look them in the eye, turn down the TV, put down your magazine).

Another thing you can do to really honor your parents is to obey them. I mentioned obedience earlier, but let's deal with it specifically. They will want you to do some things that you don't want to do. To be quite honest, you need to go ahead and do them anyway. If you always wanted to do everything they wanted you to do, then there would never be any challenge to it. The challenge is obeying even when they ask you to do things that are uncomfortable or inconvenient for you to do. We talked yesterday about bending over backward to obey the spirit of the law rather than just the letter of the law.

If your parents ask you to do some things that are blatantly against Scripture and you don't know whether you should do them or not, I encourage you to talk to your pastor or youth pastor about these things. Let them talk to your parents with you and help you work through the situation.

I want to encourage you to blow your parents away by how quickly you obey. Don't drag your feet. Don't make any negative comments.

And blow them away because you do more than they ask.

How will honoring your parents all of the time help improve the atmosphere in your home?

COMMIT TO HONOR YOUR PARENTS

The righteousness of the righteous shall be upon himself, and the wickedness of the wicked shall be upon himself.

Ezekiel 18:20

Probably the best way you can honor your parents is by showing them you are responsible. Show them that you have really learned the stuff they have been teaching you all these years. Let them see you applying their lessons to your life. Show them that your life is more together than it was and that you're beginning to prosper because you really have been listening to what they have been telling you.

Show that you are responsible by driving carefully. Do you have any tickets? Do you run red lights? Do you go faster than you should? Show that you are responsible by getting good grades. Show that you are responsible by spending your allowance or work money wisely. Do you blow it all on pizza, or are you saving some and putting it away? Don't always ask them for a handout, even for valid things like clothes or food. Show them that you are responsible by using some of your own money for necessities.

Don't be a couch potato or a slug. How do you spend your spare time? Do you play video games or sit in front of the TV all the time, or are you doing something to improve yourself and your life? You could even help out with chores around the house—without being asked. Show your mom and dad that you can be trusted. When they give you a little area of responsibility, be faithful in that so that they can give you more.

A great way to show your parents that you are responsible is to develop an accountability relationship with them as we discussed a few weeks ago. Go to them and say, "I really want to be submissive. I want to be obedient. I really want you to get in my face if you see anything in my life that's not like Jesus. I so desperately want to grow to be like Him. I know that you two are the closest people in my life, and you can see things that I may need to change." As you show yourself to be more and more responsible and mature, you will be amazed at the freedom they will give you.

As a follower of Christ, you need to make a commitment that no matter what the rest of the world does, you are going to be someone who listens to your mom and dad, respects and honors them, and submits to them, because you know that's how you'll receive God's promise of blessing.

As a follower of Christ, I commit all through my teen years to honor my parents, obey them and listen to them in everything I say and do. I refuse to walk in rebellion or in an attitude that will reflect any dishonor or disrespect to them. I want everyone to see that the way I treat my parents is the way God wants me to treat them.

______________________________ ______________

Your Signature Date

WEEK 10

COMMIT TO YOUR YOUTH GROUP AND CHURCH

REGULARLY MEET TOGETHER

Some people have gotten out of the habit of meeting for worship, but we must not do that. We should keep on encouraging each other, especially since you know that the day of the Lord's coming is getting closer.

Hebrews 10:25, *CEV*

The Bible specifically talks about the importance of getting together with other Christians so that you can learn and grow and continue going for God with all your heart. A lot of people think that after they make their commitment to the Lord, they can do whatever they want as long as they don't fall into major sin.

The point is, however, that you are not designed to be a Lone Ranger Christian—as we talked about earlier. You are designed to do incredible things for God and to change the world, but you have to be connected with other people who want to do the same thing. In Hebrews 10:25, the Bible gives you a specific instruction: "Don't you dare quit going to church! Don't you dare stop getting together with people who have a like mind and a like faith."

This is an important point for young people today. A lot of people say, "I can't make it to church. My job—my sports, my hobby, my whatever—interferes with my church and youth group." But you have to have people around you who are on fire for God the way you are. You have to surround yourself with people who love God and are going after God in the same direction.

I have talked to so many youth pastors who get really discouraged. They work their heart out for their young people, yet the young people don't seem very committed. For example, I know youth pastors who have planned and planned and planned a retreat or some other activity. They announced it for two months and mentioned it during meetings. But when it came time for the activity, no one came. It turned out that the teenagers were more committed to a school activity or sport than they were to their youth group—people with whom they are going to heaven and spending eternity.

As a follower of Christ, you need to turn that reputation around. You need to be the kind of person who says, "I know God has plugged me in here. God has a plan and a reason for my being here. I'll not commit to just Wednesday nights or just Sunday mornings. But every time that there is an opportunity for me to grow, I'm going to be here." Does that mean you have to be there every time the doors are open to church? No. But at the very least, be committed to the regular services and special events that your pastor and youth pastor have going so that they know you are a serious Christian.

I want you to take a moment and think about anything you may have done to show a lack of commitment to your youth group or to your church. Take some time this week to ask your youth pastor and pastor to forgive you for anything you have done to make their jobs more difficult. Think of some things that you can do that will show your commitment to meet with other Christians. How can you show that you have determined that you will not allow yourself to get out of the habit of meeting for worship? How can you show your commitment to your youth group and church? Don't just be a flighty, air-headed, haphazard Christian who floats in now and then.

Write down four or five ways that you can show your commitment to obey Hebrews 10:25.

____

____

____

____

____

____

____

____

Take Hebrews 10:25 and meditate on it today so that it becomes a part of your life and your heart.

PUSH EACH OTHER!

And let us consider how we may spur one another on toward love and good deeds.

Hebrews 10:24, *NIV*

If you'll notice, today's verse is the one right before the one you memorized yesterday. I want you to write out in your own words what "spur one another on toward love and good deeds" means.

One reason it's so important to regularly meet together and have a real commitment to your church and your youth group is that doing so is the way to push each other on to be more like Jesus. It's another area of accountability. We talked earlier about having accountability friendships: You need to have two or three people you are very close with. But that's not enough. You also have to be tied in to a local body of people who know your life and whose lives you know. You need to be in a place where you're being spiritually fed and you're growing, and where you're submissive to the leadership that God has put in place there. As you get into a youth group in your church, you have the opportunity to do exactly what the Scripture says: You can reignite your fire for God, really love each other and help each other do good deeds.

It's like this: God wants every youth group to be full of followers of Christ. He wants every church to be full of people who will change the world. As you grow in your commitment to your youth group and church, in effect you say to them, "I want to push you to love and good deeds. I want to help you get other new ideas on how we, as an army, can really change this world." You can't be a part of an army if you show up only now and then so that nobody can count on you. If others were counting on you but you didn't show up or you showed up without your weapon, you just blew the whole war.

As a follower of Christ, you have to decide to get plugged in and stay plugged in. You have to do everything you can to be a part of this thing. You have to say, "I'm part of the team. I'm a part of the family. I'm a part of this particular army battalion. I'm going to be a part of what God is doing here. We're going to push each other on toward love and good deeds. I'm not just going to try to push myself and spur myself on, but I'm going to let other people speak into my life and encourage other people to spur me on. We are going to be a part of a larger army, and we're going to do everything we can to find out how we can really invade and overtake this world with the love of Jesus."

List a few specific things you can do to spur on other members of your youth group.

____

____

____

____

____

____

____

____

____

REALIZE WHERE YOU BELONG

You were bought at a price; therefore glorify God in your body.

1 Corinthians 6:20

The Bible says that we have all been "bought at a price," so let's talk about what being "bought at a price" means. Jesus paid His blood for you. If you have given your heart to Him, then you don't belong to yourself anymore because He bought you. He owns you because you have freely given your life to Him. You don't give your life to Him and then live for yourself; you give your life to Him, and then you belong to Him. Think about that.

Too many young people don't really think about the fact that they belong to their youth group. They talk about how they belong to their sports teams or to the school choir or band or some other club. But they don't really talk about how they belong to their church youth group. They just go because Mom and Dad go to that church. Their identity is wrapped up in other things they do or even the cars they drive or the people they hang around with.

As a follower of Christ, you need to change your sense of belonging. I assume that if you're this far in the book, you really have given your whole life to the Lord. If this is true, then you are part of a whole group of people who also belong to the Lord. They have given their lives to God, so they belong to Him; you have given your life to God, so you belong to Him. Therefore, you belong with each other; and with them, you should find your true sense of belonging.

What does that mean? Other Christ followers, other people who are radically committed to God, are the ones you're talking about when you say, "These are my blood brothers, my blood sisters. These are the people I'm tight with. That's where my heart is, my gut is. All of my plans revolve around them. The most important thing I can do revolves around other followers of Christ, people who really want to make a difference, the people in my youth group, the people in my church who are really making a difference in the world."

When you are thinking this way, you don't look at something the church has planned and say, "I can't really do that because I have plans to go to a football game [or play soccer, go to a concert—whatever]." You change the whole thing around: "I really belong to this wild group of Christ followers who want to shake up my community and the world. If my youth group has plans to do something, I really want to participate. They are the ones I really belong to, because I'm going to be living with them forever. If they have plans, then I'll cancel anything that interferes with those plans, because my real identity is not found in football or basketball or cheerleading. My real identity is found in what we are doing for God to change this world. That's what I'm made of; that's what's eating me up on the inside; that's what I'm about! I belong with people who belong to Christ. That's where the true core of who and what I am lies."

To say that you will cancel anything that interferes is not to say that you will not be a person of your word. As a Christ follower, you have to be a man or woman of integrity. However, you may want to avoid getting involved with groups whose activities regularly conflict with your youth-group schedule. Or you could talk with your coach or other leader and tell him or her that you have a commitment to your youth group but want to participate when there's not a conflict. That would be a good way to make a strong statement about your beliefs. You definitely want to make youth-group activities a higher priority than anything like parties, dances or sporting events.

Now this is a pretty different way of thinking. Most young people "go to" youth group, but they "belong" somewhere else. Right now is the time for you to rethink why you are in a youth group. If you really love God as you say, then you need to start pouring your energy into the things that your youth group and church are trying to accomplish.

Make a list of things that you feel you belong to or that you are really tight with right now.

How do you think you can change your sense of belonging so that you're more committed to your youth group and to your church than the other things?

Make a decision today to get more committed to your youth group and your church and to feel more at home there than you do anywhere else, because you're with people who belong together as people bought at a price by Jesus.

DAY 4

TAKE UP THE VISION

Whatever you do, do it heartily, as to the Lord and not to men.

Colossians 3:23

God knows that all people long to find something they can do generously, compassionately and enthusiastically, with their whole heart and mind. I think one of the biggest problems today is that young people are trying to find something to pour their lives and their guts into, but they can't seem to find something to give their all for. Some teens pour their lives into academics or the pursuit of a career. Some get involved in sports or other worthwhile activities, but some get caught up in drugs or gang activity. Although all of these interests and activities may not seem to have anything in common, they all are examples of the wide variety of distractions available for teens. They distract from the main thing we were designed to pour our hearts into: the things of God and what He has called us to do.

We humans have a built-in tendency to pour our lives into something, and the Bible tells us exactly what that something should be: "Love the Lord your God with all your heart, soul and strength" (see Mark 12:30). You ought to pour your life into the things of God. Yes, you can be involved in other interests for fun, but He wants your heart to be in helping to promote His kingdom. He knows that when you pour your life into it, you'll be the most fulfilled.

Let me get more specific. God has given you a church and a youth group for a reason. He has given your youth pastor and pastor a vision for what they want to do to shake up and change your city, your town, your area, your region. It is absolutely imperative for you as a follower of Christ to become involved with the vision that your youth pastor and pastor have for your youth group and your church to shake up the world. They have to know that your heart is there, your guts are there, your soul is there. You want to do everything you can to blow that thing wide open and to make it awesome and totally successful. You want to show the world that God is doing something through your youth group. It has to have your identity, your sense of belonging.

You need to say, "The sweetest thing God is doing in town, next to my quiet time, is what God is doing in my youth group. We're shaking up the city. We're invading every place people go to hang out. We're turning over the junior high. We're turning over the senior high. We're strategically intervening at all the sports games to cause revival at halftime. We're doing stuff that really makes a difference. It's not just that I'm sort of involved or I come when the youth pastor begs me. I'm there before he wants me there, and I'm praying for it and planning for it. I'm taking notes, and I'm volunteering my time because I'm committed with all of my heart to this vision that God has given my youth pastor and my pastor. In fact, I have taken it on as my own. It's not just their vision; it's my vision because I'm a part of this church and this youth group. I'm going to pour my guts into doing everything I can to make this happen."

You need to take some time to meet with your youth pastor (and maybe your pastor, depending on how busy he or she is) and ask where you fit into the vision. Explain that you have some free time, and you want to really pour your life into this thing. Ask for clear directions about what help you can be to further that vision. Explain that you want to be more than an attendee: You want to be someone whose heart, soul and guts are totally sold out to this thing.

Memorize Colossians 3:23 today. Meditate on it and chew on it all day long. Then schedule an appointment with your youth pastor.

List some things that you can do to further the vision of your youth group or church.

____

____

____

Do those things with all your heart, and you will have so much fulfillment that you won't know what to do with yourself.

One more thing for you to think about: If you are genuinely committed to the vision, you give and tithe to your youth group and church each week. If you are really pouring your heart into it, your money will naturally follow. And if you give and tithe to your local fellowship, God will bless you for it.

DAY 5

SUBMIT TO GOVERNING AUTHORITIES (PART 1: YOUR YOUTH PASTOR)

Everyone must submit himself to the governing authorities, for there is no authority except that which God has established. The authorities that exist have been established by God.

Romans 13:1, *NIV*

As a follower of Christ, you have to be committed to the vision of your youth group and your church, and you need to be specifically committed to your youth pastor and loyal to him or her. I mentioned a few days ago that many youth pastors feel discouraged. They're doing this thing called youth ministry, and they feel like they have to drag all the young people along with them.

A follower doesn't have to be dragged. A follower drags other people along to jump into what the youth pastor is doing. A follower of Christ is not someone who mocks the youth pastor and lets him worship all by himself or preach all by himself while everyone else is drifting off. A follower bends over backward to be submissive to the youth pastor.

A lot of the same principles that I talked about regarding showing submission and respect to your parents also apply to your youth pastor. If he asks you to stop talking, you don't start writing notes instead. In fact, you shouldn't have been talking in the first place. You should be bending over backward to show your self as an example to others of the kind of attitude they should have toward the youth pastor. You don't want to be talking behind his back. You don't want to be running him down into the ground. You don't want to be whispering malicious rumors about him or your dislike of certain things he does. If there is something you dislike about what he has said, then be honest enough to go to him face to face. If he changes his mind, fine. If he doesn't, say,

"I'm committed to this vision. I'm committed to you. I'm going to shut my mouth and go along with this." It takes a big man or woman to realize and live with disagreements. God has given you this leader, and you need to submit to this authority.

When you are loyal to your youth pastor, you show that you believe that God has placed you in that group, that God has placed him or her over you, and that you are going to listen to and follow your youth pastor with a great attitude.

Being respectful to your youth pastor means you're going to honor him and obey him. It means you'll listen to him. You're going to take notes about his preaching. You're going to worship. It doesn't mean that you have to agree with everything. But you will be wholeheartedly committed to his vision. Being respectful and loyal to your youth pastor means that when there is a school activity and a youth group activity at the same time, you choose what he has organized rather than a school activity.

I know that sounds dramatic and over the edge, but it should be part of your typical behavior. God's activities are more important than any school activity, but a lot of people just go to a youth group because their moms and dads go to that church.

A Christ follower has a different attitude, though. You don't just go there because your mom and dad go to that church. You go to the youth group because God has His plan in this whole thing. God put you there as a part of that group, and God put that leader there in charge of you. By honoring that leader, you are honoring God. God will bless your life, and you will be amazed at how much leadership you will develop by learning to really follow and submit.

You can find many examples in the Scriptures. For example, in Acts 16:3, when Paul wanted to take Timothy along on a journey, Paul circumcised him because the Jews who lived in that area knew Timothy's father was Greek. Timothy submitted to Paul even to the point of being circumcised, even though it was clear that no one was saved by circumcision. Wow! If he could do that, surely you can submit to your youth pastor and pastor. What they want you to do would never be that drastic! The leaders who are over different areas of your life are there because God put them there. Now it's time to wholeheartedly respect and honor them. Respect and honor your youth pastor because he or she has been placed there by God.

List some things that you may have done that showed dishonor to or disrespect of your youth leader.

List some incredible things that you will do this week to show the youth pastor that you are going to honor, listen to and obey him or her from this point forward.

Take a few minutes now to memorize Romans 13:1. Make the appointment with your youth pastor this week to ask her to forgive you in any areas where you have dishonored her. Ask her how you can get plugged in to the vision. Tell her of your commitment to the vision.

SUBMIT TO GOVERNING AUTHORITIES (PART 2: YOUR SENIOR PASTOR)

He who rebels against the authority is rebelling against what God has instituted, and those who do so will bring judgment on themselves.

Romans 13:2, *NIV*

A follower of Christ is respectful of the senior pastor and the entire leadership of the church (the elders and other leaders). Everything doesn't just all revolve around your youth group. You are also a member of your church at large. If you're really going to be a Christ follower, you need to know how to display the right kind of attitude toward your pastor.

Sometimes when young people attend worship services, they come to church with an attitude that is disrespectful to the leaders of the church and to the pastor himself. Too many young people think, *My youth pastor can relate to me, but the pastor of my church is old and can't really relate.* They mock him or pass notes in the back row. The attitude of a follower should be completely different from that. God will not permit you to be that way. If you want God to bless your life, you need to honor leadership and authority at every level He gives you. Your pastor is one of the leaders.

You can do some specific things to show your pastor honor and respect. Sit in the front row instead of the back row. Join in the worship service. Look the pastor right in the eye when he looks at you. On the way out of church, shake the pastor's hand and say, "Pastor, I appreciate you. Thank you for speaking into my life."

Take notes while you listen to the sermon, and try to get a lot out of the message. If you open up your heart and pray, *God, please help me to really listen to what You are speaking to me today,* you'll be amazed at what God will speak through your pastor, even though the pastor may be a lot older than you. After all, the Word of God is thousands of years old, and it still relates to you. So what if your pastor is older than you? The two of you can still relate to each other.

You can also show respect to your pastor by the way you dress. A lot of young people come to church dressed as if they're going to hang out with their friends. God doesn't care what you look like on the outside, but your appearance can show an attitude of respect or disrespect. Think about it this way: If you were going to meet with the president of the United States or some other country, how would you dress? Would you dress like a slob and have messy hair?

As I've traveled to churches around the country, I've seen many young people sloppily dressed and with what looks like uncombed hair. It's true that we're going to the house of God to meet with the Lord Almighty; and, of course, He looks at our hearts, not our outward appearance. But we should care enough about the way we carry ourselves that we look at least a little respectful. Does that mean you have to wear a shirt and tie or a dress every time? No. But maybe you should try it at least now and then. Care about how you carry yourself and put yourself together, because how you dress communicates to the pastor and the entire church congregation whether or not they're important to you. Honor the pastor by how you carry yourself and how you look.

List some things you will do this week to begin to show your pastor and other church leaders that you honor and respect them.

DAY 7

COMMIT TO YOUR YOUTH GROUP AND CHURCH

Don't let anyone make fun of you, just because you are young. Set an example for other followers by what you say and do, as well as by your love, faith, and purity.

1 Timothy 4:12, *CEV*

The Bible encourages you not to let anyone mock or look down on you just because you're young. Some people mock teenage Christians and don't take them seriously. Some older people might think that the teens look and dress like slobs, like they're not very committed—they are up and down and back and forth; They're on fire, falling away, on fire, falling way.

As a follower of Christ, you want to change that image. You want to show people that you are part of a force to be reckoned with. You are serious about God, your Christian life and your commitment to your youth group and church.

In 1 Timothy 4:12, Paul tells Timothy to be an example of faith, purity and love. In other words, young people should be blowing the adults away. The adults should look at the teens in the youth group and say to themselves, *Wow! Why am I not loving people like that? Why don't I have that much respect for my pastor? Why am I not that committed to my church?* Young people should be an example to everyone else. Others should be imitating, not mocking, the youth group.

As a follower of Christ, you need to get a new picture of what your commitment to your youth group and church and to your youth pastor and senior pastor really looks like. This is not a haphazard, only-when-it's-convenient thing. Come rain or shine, you're going to church. If the postal carrier can get out in the rain, shine, snow and sleet, why can't you go to church? You might say, *Oh yes,*

Lord, I'll die for You; I'll do anything for You. But then it gets a little rainy outside, and you don't go to church because you might get your hair messy. Hey, that's bogus! You need to have the kind of commitment that says, "I'm going to show myself as an example! I don't care if I have to walk the whole way through five miles of rain and mud and sleet and hail. I'm going to be there because my heart is there, my guts are there, my commitment is there, my life is there. God has called me to this thing, and I'm pouring my life into it."

Make a commitment today that even though you're young, you'll live the kind of life and have the kind of commitment to your church and youth group that people will look at and say, "Wow! What an incredible example!"

List some things that you can do or are already doing that will be an example for people to follow.

As a follower of Christ, I commit all of my teen years to my youth group, to my church, to my youth pastor, to my pastor and to other church leaders, because I know that it is no accident that I am here. I know that God has given me these leaders and these groups to be involved with to help me grow and to help me change the world. Lord, I commit to find my part in the vision of my youth group and my church and to do everything I can with all my heart to be a part of it.

Your Signature

Date

WEEK 11

BE THE ONE TO START A REVOLUTION

LOVE GOD WITH ALL YOUR STRENGTH

Love the Lord your God with all your heart, with all your soul, with all your mind, and with all your strength.

Mark 12:30

Although we've been talking about loving God all through this book, this week we're going to talk specifically about loving God with all of your strength—that is, using your energy and your power to really do something for God. What does it mean to love the Lord your God with all your strength? Write out in your own words what you think it means.

____

____

____

____

____

In today's verse, Jesus says, "Listen, if you really love God with everything you've got, it ought to affect the way you use your strength!" Think about the way you use your strength, or your energy, right now. Do you use your energy to expand the kingdom of God? Obviously, in these last few weeks, you've been using a lot of energy to grow in the Lord—and that's great. But now it's time to think about how to use your energy as a follower of Christ to really do something to change the world.

People have been talking about changing the world for a long time. They've been thinking about it; they've got plans for it; they've got processes for it and statistics about it. Actually, they've been doing everything but changing the world. It's time for you, as a young maniac who loves God, to start thinking about how you can use your power and energy to love Him to change this world—to start a revolution.

Loving God with all your strength means that while you have strength, while you're alive on this earth, you will make a commitment. You will use the bulk of your energy for God. Don't let your energy get sapped by other interests. Use your energy to love God! Find ways to kick the devil in the face, and do something about starting a revolution to change the world. You will do something that will kick in the doors of hell and let people know that God is alive inside of you!

Too many people, maybe even you, use so much of their energy for things that don't give glory to God. They may be doing activities that don't seem to do anyone any harm, but they are certainly not working to expand the kingdom of God; their activities don't do anything of value. God knows that the way for you to have the most exciting and fulfilling life is for you to pour your guts and your sweat into loving Him and showing the world that you love Him by what you do.

Think of several things you can do with your energy this week that will show the world your love for Him. Realize that you're not trying to do anything to earn His love because He already loves you so much that He just blows you away with His love. It's the natural response to His love to want to do something out of gratitude for what He's done for you.

List a few things that you could do this week that will show the world you love God.

____

____

____

____

____

____

Start doing these things today.

STEP OUT

Jonathan said to his young armor-bearer, "Come, let's go over to the outpost of those uncircumcised fellows. Perhaps the LORD will act in our behalf. Nothing can hinder the Lord from saving, whether by many or by few."

1 Samuel 14:6, *NIV*

Jonathan's words recorded in 1 Samuel 14:6 show that he was committed to starting a revolution. Here he was, involved in a battle where he and six hundred other men were surrounded by the Philistines, and everything looked bad. The Philistines had kept the Israelites from making weapons—in the whole army, only King Saul and his son, Jonathan, had weapons. As you can imagine, the men in the army were getting so discouraged that they were beginning to give up hope.

Then in the midst of all these problems, Jonathan got this holy itch. Something began to stir inside him, and he said to himself, *I can't just sit here and do nothing. I can't sit here and watch the devil run all over us. Who do these people think they are? We are the army of the living God! Man, I've got to do something about this!*

Let me ask you: Do you have a holy itch today? As you experience peer pressure at school and see the devil run all over people's lives—sometimes even so badly that the Christians look like so many losers shoved in a corner—do you get mad enough to want to do something? Do you have a holy itch? Do you say to yourself, *I can't stand the way things are, and I've got to do something about it*?

Jonathan did something! He got his armor bearer and said, "Let's go and at least look at these guys and see how big their army is. Perhaps the Lord will act in our behalf. Nothing can hinder the Lord from saving." Jonathan had an attitude that said, "Just maybe, just perhaps on the slight possibility that God could blow our minds and do something incredible, let's go look at these guys."

Do you have such faith and conviction? It's time for young people to stand up tall and say, "In Jesus' name, I have faith and I have conviction that God is on my side. Just perhaps God will use me to set my campus on fire. Perhaps God will use me, and revival will break out during halftime at a ball game. Maybe God will use me, and revival will break out in my cafeteria when I stand up to share Christ. Just perhaps God will use me to cause my youth group to explode. Perhaps God will use me to invade another country and get people saved all around the world. Just maybe in the midst of a war that looks like the devil is winning, just maybe God will use me." You need to have the heart and soul of a revolutionary inside of you.

Meditate and chew on 1 Samuel 14:6 as you walk through your school's hallways today. Meditate on how God will use you. Pray like crazy for God to give you the holy itch that makes you totally uncomfortable watching people around you who are going to hell, that makes you have to do something about it!

The United States Constitution guarantees your freedom of speech, so you have the right to speak in public places, including in school. Just make sure whatever you do is tactful and will be a positive witness for Jesus. Think of a couple of situations at school where you could share the good news about Jesus.

DAY 3

CHANGE YOUR REPUTATION

These who have turned the world upside down have come here too.

Acts 17:6

Paul and his band of followers had a reputation as they traveled from town to town. As they were brought to court before the officials, this accusation was made against them. Everyone knew their reputation. Everywhere they went, they turned things upside down. They ruffled feathers and stirred things up. They refused to go unnoticed. They never left anything the way it had been before they arrived. Paul had this thing inside him that said, "I cannot stand by and let the devil run this world and mess up people's lives. I don't care what it costs me. I don't care what people say about me or do to me. I have to do something about the evil in this world."

Think about what your Christian friends and your non-Christian friends would say about you if they were put on a witness stand and had to account for the kind of Christian you are. What kind of reputation would they say you have? What would they say about the way you live your Christian life?

____

____

____

____

____

As you grow in your commitment to be a follower of Christ, this is your chance to change your reputation. Now is your chance to be the kind of Christian that you've always wanted to be. Now is the time to get out of your comfort zone. To make a difference—to change the world—you're going to have to ruffle some feathers. It's time to take a stand and be counted. It's time, not just to shake things up for the sake of shaking them up, but to shake things up so that people's lives can be changed. Bring people to the realization that they can enter into an incredible relationship with Jesus. Decide that you're sick of the status quo, and determine to do something about it. You've been intimidated by the devil and people's opinions way too long.

We have all seen a watered-down Christianity that says that to go to heaven, all you have to do is go to church, pay a tithe and die. But that's not the way it is everywhere. You can join those who have realized it is time to stand up and say, "I'm going to make my life count. I'm going to do something to change this world."

List some things you can do right now to turn things upside down at your school and work and in the lives of people you hang out with.

If in six months you could have any kind of reputation in terms of doing something for God, what would you like people to say about you?

Now is your chance to change your actions so that they will line up with what you really want people to see in you. You can become the kind of Christian who makes a difference in a very real way. Decide today what you'll do to make this difference and to gain the reputation that you really want to have.

DAY 4

WRITE THE VISION

Then the Lord answered me and said: "Write the vision and make it plain on tablets, that he may run who reads it."

Habakkuk 2:2

Take a few minutes right now to memorize this verse.

Now that you're stirred up and you've got that holy itch—that you're determined to turn the world upside down wherever you go—it's time to really crystallize your vision. Ask God, *What do You want to do through me and with me? How do You want to use me now in my school and in my community? What do You want to do with me through my job, sports, clubs and youth group? What's Your vision for me, Lord?*

Most young people go from day to day, week to week, and year to year never really thinking, *How does God want to use me right now, while I'm young?* God will begin to speak to you as you continue to get the Word down into your heart. As you continue having your quiet times, praying like crazy and committing to live a holy life, God promises He will speak to you. He said, "My sheep know My voice" (see John 10:4).

He'll speak to you and give you a vision. It's important for you to write the vision down as it says in Habakkuk 2:2. Don't just say, "Well, I think I'll live for God today and do something cool." You have to write it down. You have to make it plain: What do I want to do for God my freshman year, my sophomore year, my junior year, and my senior year? What do I want to do with my summers? Maybe I could go on missions trips, go to the inner city, or really minister and change people's lives here in my own community. What do I want to do in my sports life and my friends' lives and my social life?

You've already talked to your youth pastor about the vision of your youth group. Now you need to find out the answers to these questions: *God, what part of that vision belongs to me? What do*

You want me to do? Part of your vision should definitely be a part of what God is doing through your youth group.

You shouldn't be stumbling through your teen years and your Christian life thinking, *One day I'll grow up, and then I'll really get my vision.* Right now, your vision should be what gives you zest in life, what you lose sleep over, what you can't wait to get up for the next day. What does God want to do in your life, and how does He want to use you to change the world?

You need to stop right now. Slow down and ask, "God, what is Your vision for me? What is Your vision for my sophomore year, my senior year, my freshman year in college? If You could do everything possible through me, what would my school look like in six months? What would my youth group look like in six months if You could do everything You wanted through me? What would my ball team look like in six months or a year? God, if You really could use me and do anything, what would it look like?"

Now I want you to begin to dream. Just imagine and write out your thoughts here. What would your job look like, your ball team, all the different facets of your life? What would your teachers look like? How many of them would have gotten saved? How many of your counselors, advisors, or school administrators would have gotten saved? Dare to imagine and to dream big, and then write that vision down so that you have something specific to aim for.

DAY 5

BE COMPELLED TO SPEAK

Yet when I preach the gospel, I cannot boast, for I am compelled to preach. Woe to me if I do not preach the gospel!

1 Corinthians 9:16, *NIV*

In today's verse, Paul described what was going on inside his heart and soul: "This thing that is burning inside is so real and so alive, I have to speak it. I have to preach it. I have to get what's inside of me out so that others can hear it." As a follower of Christ, you should have a life and a relationship with Jesus so real and so alive that something burns inside of you, something that has to come out.

What you have inside of you is an encounter with the living God! This is an encounter with the God who forgave you and gave you a new heart, a new mind and a new life. This is an encounter with the God who made the whole earth. He has totally, radically and forever changed you on the inside. You have a new heart and a new spirit. For the very first time, you have a real life! After Paul was similarly changed, he said, "This thing is so real inside of me, it's so alive, I've got to get it out. I don't care what people say. I don't care what people do. I've got to start a revolution." And that's exactly what he did. As he went from town to town, he started a revolution and a fire, and he stirred people up.

As a follower of Christ, you've got to journey through life with the same conviction. You're not just another cheese-ball Christian sitting in a pew. You're not just another young person in a youth group somewhere. You've got this thing burning inside of you! It's an encounter with God. You can barely describe it in human words, but it's a miracle that has happened inside of you.

I want to encourage you to begin your day with the same kind of attitude that Paul had. Take five minutes to meditate on 1 Corinthians 9:16. Memorize it, and chew on it. Take it with you all day long. Let this be your motto for today and for this week: "This thing is so real to me, I've got to do something. If I don't say something, this thing will eat me alive!"

Write out some things that you can do today that will really express what you've got inside of you that just has to come out. (In other words, tell what you can say to and do with the people you know you are going to see today to help them understand what you've got living and beating inside your heart.)

____

____

____

____

____

____

____

____

____

Now launch forth with boldness and courage as Paul did. Live life with the conviction that says, "If I don't get some of what's inside of me into someone else, I don't know if I'll be able to make it through the day." If you believe and act on that with all your heart, you'll change the world.

BE A REVOLUTIONARY

Then He called His twelve disciples together and gave them power and authority over all demons, and to cure diseases. He sent them to preach the kingdom of God and to heal the sick.

Luke 9:1-2

As a follower of Christ, you need to see yourself as a revolutionary. Sure, once in a while, you'll see people witnessing and sharing their faith with other people; but they're the exception to the rule. Too many Christians aren't like that. You, however, are a world changer, and you need to change what the average Christian looks like.

True Christians, according to Jesus' definition, are people who are moving and shaking and stirring things up. Jesus' disciples were examples of people who lived this way. One time He sent them off to villages and towns to cast out demons, heal the sick and share the gospel of the kingdom of God. But before they left, He told them:

> Take nothing for the journey, neither staff nor bag nor bread nor money; and do not have two tunics apiece. Whatever house you enter, stay there, and from there depart and whoever will not receive you, when you go out of that city, shake off the very dust from your feet as a testimony against them (Luke 9:3-5).

Then He brought them back to talk about what they had done. Later He sent about 70 others to preach, minister and share. He was so radical, He told them not to take anything with them, just as He had told the original disciples:

> After these things the Lord appointed seventy others also, and sent them two by two before His face into every city

> and place where He Himself was about to go. Then He said to them, "The harvest truly is great, but the laborers are few; therefore pray the Lord of the harvest to send out laborers into His harvest. Go your way; behold, I send you out as lambs among wolves. Do not take purse or bag or sandals; and greet no one along the road (Luke 10:1-4).

They, like the original 12 disciples had done, all came back amazed by the power they had been able to exhibit. And they had done it all by letting God supply what they needed. Then Jesus told His disciples:

> Go therefore and make disciples of all the nations, baptizing them in the name of the Father and of the Son and of the Holy Spirit (Matthew 28:19).

You see, this lifestyle of a follower of Christ, this lifestyle of being a revolutionary and turning things upside down just like Jesus did, is not optional. And it's not like just some people who are really on fire should do this, and all the rest should sit in the back pew.

God intends for everyone who joins His army to be involved in a fiery, passionate, committed way in order to make a difference in the world. It's not just the preachers like Billy Graham who can make a difference. All of us get to make a difference. The thing that makes a difference inside is not just saying, "Okay, I'm going to go make a difference." It's the fact that something has really changed your life. The lifestyle that God wants you to take on is somehow transmitting what He has done inside you into another person.

When Jesus sent the disciples out the last time, He told them not to come back. In other words, this is the kind of life God wants you to lead. This is the kind of life He wants you to live. This is what your habit should be. This is what you should be doing. And this should be normal! This should be what every Christian is doing, because this is what Jesus commanded all His disciples to do.

Write Luke 9:1-2 out on an index card, and take it with you today. I want you to think about what the lifestyle of a true disciple of Jesus should be. I want you to chew on it and think about it all day long. Begin to imagine yourself having that kind of lifestyle.

You're a revolutionary. You're a Christ follower. You're going to live on the edge just like those guys did. If you have to take nothing with you, you'll do it. Refuse to fit into the mold of a boring Christian. Step out on the edge and live a lifestyle of doing something to affect this world for Jesus.

List some things that you can do right now to turn things upside down at your school and/or work. How about in the lives of people you hang out with?

DAY 7

COMMIT TO START A REVOLUTION

How can I [understand], unless someone guides me?

Acts 8:31

As you think about living the lifestyle of a revolutionary, the lifestyle of a follower of Christ, there's one huge question you need to ask yourself. But first, I want you to consider the confidence you have in your relationship with God. *I know God changed my life. I remember the day I gave my life and my heart to Him. I know the areas of my life He has cleaned up. I know how much He has spoken to me. I know that as He has spoken to me, my life has been changed.*

As you've worked your way through this book, maybe you've been aware that God is dealing with you in different areas of your life—you've given up some problem things, and you're experiencing freedom from the bondage you were in. That's great! That's incredible! That's exactly what I've been praying for you!

Now the question you need to ask yourself is this: *How do I get what happened in me—in my relationship with God—to happen in somebody else?* This is the question of the ages. How do we help others to really get connected to God in a way that causes them to fall on their knees and completely convert their lives over to God? This is my life's dream. This is what beats in my heart. This is what I think about all the time. As I'm sitting next to someone on a plane, as I'm preaching to a crowd of people in a developing country and as I'm preaching to thousands of people every weekend at Acquire the Fire conventions, I ask myself this question: *How do I get kids, teenagers, people from another nation, or people who live in a village somewhere to get really connected with God so that God totally blows their minds and changes their lives the way He did mine?*

I believe that this is a question for every person who really wants to change the world. We don't want to get people chanting meaningless prayers. It's easy to get people to raise their hands and pray, "Lord Jesus, come into my heart." But too many who have done that seem to live the same way they did before. An evangelist can come into town. The leaders can play the music just right, have the choir singing and people coming forward. The lighting can be just right. People can cry and pray a prayer. But none of it is any good if the people don't really get connected with God.

After you've ministered to somebody and you leave, is that person still connected with God? Has that person had a real heart-to-heart, face-to-face, blow-your-mind, never-the-same experience with God? Sometimes I ask, "God, how did You do it inside me? I was a total heathen. I didn't want You. I was messed up on drugs. My life was being flushed down the toilet. How did You get through to me? Why was it so real to me? What can I possibly say or do to help someone else understand it?"

So many times when we begin to tell people about the Lord, we get into a rut. We mumble, "Well, you know, I . . ." Or we get the Four Spiritual Laws tract out and start reciting it. Or we start saying, "All have sinned and fall short of the glory of God. And you know, the wages of sin is death . . ." These are true and these are real, but how do we get the miracle that happened inside us to happen inside other people?

I don't know. I think people can say to themselves, *Yes, I give my life to Jesus,* and still live the same way they lived before and never really get anything done. I believe that true followers of Christ—people who want to stir things up, ruffle feathers and cause a revolution—have to be creative about how they get the gospel to other people.

You have to be creative about how you communicate, what you say and what you do. Every day, as you are reading the Bible and seeking God, He'll share stuff with you. Keep that stuff in your coat pocket, just like a bunch of daggers, so that you've got something to—*Boom! Boom! Boom!*—hit people with. These will be things that just blow their minds. "Wow, where'd you hear that?" they'll ask. "I heard from God!" you'll answer.

God will share that kind of stuff with you. But you have to be creative. I want you to take a few moments and write out some creative ways that you can start a revolution in your school. Write out some creative ways that you can communicate the gospel. If you were going to communicate the gospel to someone who worked at McDonald's, how would you communicate it to him? If you were going to communicate the gospel to someone on your football team, how would you say it in a creative way? How would you creatively share the gospel with someone in your chemistry class?

I'm not advocating breaking laws or school rules, but there is still a lot you can do for good without violating the rules. Remember, the most important thing here is not a little cheese-ball message. It is somehow getting into words the miracle that has happened in your heart so that others can glimpse it.

Take some time now and write down some creative scenarios for different situations you may find yourself in.

Now commit today to start a revolution and communicate the gospel in a creative ways, trying to put into words what has happened to you.

As a follower of Christ, I commit to start a revolution. I commit to do something to get the gospel out right where I live. I will turn this world upside down, and I'll start with my school and this town. I commit to have a reputation like Paul had. I refuse to sit down and watch people go to hell as I just live my life. I have to do something to make a difference, and I have to start doing something today.

______________________________ ____________

Your Signature Date

WEEK 12

The Adventure of a Lifetime

DAY 1

PRAY!

The harvest is great, but the laborers are few; therefore pray the Lord of the harvest to send out laborers into His harvest.

Luke 10:2

As a follower of Christ, you want to really change the world. You don't just want to change your community. You're not just committed to ministering to people and stirring up a revolution in your state, region or country. You want to do something that actually changes the world.

Jesus told His disciples to pray, and this wasn't a casual suggestion. He said, "Pray! I mean pray your faces off! I mean let it get under your skin. Feel the heartbeat of God as He cares for the people around the world. Pray that God will raise up laborers, people who will go. Start having a little compassion in your heart about the things that God has compassion in His heart about, and pray that God will send people."

Sometimes when you pray for the people of the world, you pray a five-second prayer like, "God, please bless those missionaries in China. In Jesus' name, amen." Wow, did God move in that prayer or what? No, God wants you to really begin to care about the people of the world. He wants you to care enough to do something. The first step is to pray. I mean really pray. Take a book like *Operation World* by Patrick Johnstone and read about different countries. Pray for the unreached people groups in each country. Pray for the people who have never, ever had a chance to hear the gospel even if they wanted to, because there is no one to tell them about this Lord in whom we say we believe.

As you and thousands of other young people pledge a commitment to become followers, your first point of contact to change other parts of the world besides your neighborhood is to pray. Pray for remote areas. Pray for the missionaries your church supports. Find out everything you can learn about your missionaries and their countries, and pray your face off for them. Look in the encyclopedia, if nothing else, and pray for countries and people who have never had a chance to hear about Jesus. Pray until you feel God's broken heart for them. Pray until you weep and you feel the compassion of God rising up in your heart. Pray that God will raise up people to do something about the tragedy that is happening to millions of people all over the world who have never had a chance to hear about Jesus, like the AIDS orphans in Liberia or the atrocity of the sex-trafficking in Thailand.

Prayers for the world should be a part of your regular quiet time. Don't just pray about yourself. Don't just pray for your immediate situation that day. Instead, begin to pray for unreached people around the world on a regular basis so that your heart is not just for America but for all countries. You will begin to get a glimpse of the world the way God sees it. God cares about all people—including the unreached—and He said that He is not coming back until all people get a chance to hear about Him: "And this gospel of the kingdom will be preached in all the world as a witness to all the nations, and then the end will come" (Matthew 24:14).

So the first step today is to become involved in praying for people around the world who never have had a chance to hear the gospel. Take some time right now and pray for an unreached people group in a different country from your own.

What missionaries do your church support? Where are they working? How can you support them and encourage them?

____

____

____

____

____

____

____

____

GO!

Go! I am sending you out like lambs among wolves.

Luke 10:3, *NIV*

Did you notice that in the Bible, today's verse immediately follows yesterday's verse? Isn't it interesting that in one sentence Jesus told the disciples to pray with their hearts for people to go, and then in the next sentence He told the very same people to go? Basically, He told them that they needed to start being the answer to their own prayer. He didn't want them just to sit there and do nothing. He wanted them to go and do something.

Don't be a part of that group of people who just pray and talk about things. Put some legs on your prayer, and do something about it. He said, "Go!" with an exclamation point. It was not a casual suggestion. It was a thundering imperative: "Go!"

Jesus was trying to help the disciples understand that it needed to be a lifestyle. This is not just an opportunity for God to change you. It is an opportunity for you to stir yourself up to go and do something different from the average person who believes.

"Go" indicates a change of location. It implies movement. Jesus said, "I am sending you out like lambs among wolves." In other words, "I know that you are lambs. You are not even sheep yet. You're young. You're not very old and not very strong yet, but I want you to go anyway."

Some young people think, *How can I go? I am just a teenager. How can God use me?* This is the very point that Jesus addressed here. He said, "You are young. You may not have my knowledge of everything godly. You're wet behind the ears—maybe you feel as if you don't have much between your ears—but go anyway."

Maybe you don't feel like a very strong Christian. Maybe you don't feel as if there is much substance to your Christian life. Maybe you haven't memorized very many Scriptures. (But you have memorized all the Scriptures in this book so far!) Maybe you don't feel like the best preacher in the world. Maybe you don't even know if you are going to be a missionary for the rest of your life. That is okay. Jesus sent guys out a couple of times, and many of them came back to Jerusalem and lived there. He said, "I want you to go at least one time because once you have gone, you'll never be the same. Even though you are young, I want you to go."

You may be going through this devotional and you're only 13 or 14 years old. That's great! Jesus said, "You might be a lamb—you might be young—but go anyway." He didn't say, "I'm going to use you, even though you are so young." I think the point is that *because you are young*, you are still flexible enough and willing to live on the edge enough to really be used to do something that will change the world.

It is time to blow the excuses out of your head. You are never too young to go. My wife and I have been taking our kids overseas since they were one and two years old. They go every year, and they look forward to it. God uses the trip to change their lives. Don't let your age keep you back from doing something great and changing the world while you're young.

Begin to pray right now:

> *God, You said in Your Word that Jesus told them to go, even though they were young, even though they were lambs. God, where do You want me to go? What do You want me to do? What country should I go to? Which people could You use me to bring the gospel to? I want to follow Jesus' instruction to "go into all the world and preach the gospel to every creature" [Mark 16:15]. Please tell me where I can be of use. In Jesus' name, amen.*

Pray that prayer every day, and listen to God as He speaks to your heart.

CHANGE THE WORLD WHILE YOU'RE YOUNG

When this had dawned on him, he went to the house of Mary, the mother of John, also called Mark, where many people had gathered and were praying.

Acts 12:12, *NIV*

I want to tell you about an incredible example from Scripture of a young man who changed the world. His name was John Mark. Read Acts 12:1-17 for the story of Peter's escape from prison through the miraculous work of an angel.

When Peter realized that he was actually out of prison—that it wasn't a dream—he knocked on the door of a house where a bunch of believers were meeting. He went to the house of Mary, the mother of John also called Mark, where people had gathered and were praying. After some confusion, they let him in the house and realized that it was a miracle. One person in the house was a young man named John Mark. He was maybe 13 or 14 years old. He got to hear firsthand how Peter was busted out of jail by an angel.

Now read what it says just a few verses later:

> When Barnabas and Saul had finished their mission, they returned from Jerusalem, taking with them John also called Mark (Acts 12:25, *NIV*).

So John Mark saw this miracle of Peter being busted out of jail, and before he knew it, he went on a mission trip with Paul and Barnabas. He is an incredible example of a young man who went as a teenager to hang out with Paul and Barnabas on their adventures. He watched them preach the gospel, get thrown in jail, preach the gospel and get whipped. He helped Paul and Barnabas start churches all over the place:

> When they arrived in Salamis, they preached the word of God in the synagogues of the Jews. They also had John as their assistant (Acts 13:5).

There he was helping them, standing with them, ministering with them, assisting them in any way he could. It is time to do something while you're young just like this young champion John Mark did. This young John Mark is the same Mark who eventually wrote the gospel of Mark. He wrote the whole book from his perspective as a teenager. He started while he was young changing the world and doing incredible things.

What would have happened if John Mark's mom or dad had said, "No, you're too young to go on that mission trip"? Maybe the book of Mark would never have been written. What would have happened if John Mark had said, "Well, that was a really cool miracle with Peter, but I don't know about going with Paul and Barnabas. That seems too scary. I heard that they have been in jail. I heard that they get rocks thrown at them when they preach"? But John Mark did not let anything intimidate him. You, as a young follower of Christ today, cannot let anything intimidate you. Just imagine the incredible things that you could do, things that God wants to start doing through you right now—while you're young.

I want you to keep praying:

> *God, where do You want me to go? God, what do You want me to do, even this summer? God, could You use me for a week or a couple of weeks in another country? Could You use me a month or two months somewhere while I am young? God, use me to change the world while I am young like You used John Mark. Help me set a healthy pattern of living the lifestyle of a follower of Christ to keep for the rest of my life. In Jesus' name, amen.*

DAY 4

FULFILL THE GREAT COMMISSION

Go therefore and make disciples of all the nations, baptizing them in the name of the Father and of the Son and of the Holy Spirit.

Matthew 28:19

Take four minutes and memorize this Scripture. Copy it down and carry it with you all day long. This passage of Scripture is called the Great Commission. It is God's mandate for you as a follower of Christ. He calls you to do whatever you have to do to make your life count for reaching the world. He has not called just a few people to go, and this is not called "the Great Suggestion." This commission is for anybody who calls on the name of Christ.

If you are part of the army of Christ, then you have to be involved in the battle. The battle is on the front lines helping people to hear the gospel who have never heard it before. Your job is to push back the enemy territory. This is not an option. It is not just a good idea for only a few people to take up and do something about. This is for everybody. I believe with all my heart that every single person should go at least one time to take the gospel to another country.

You should go while you're young. You know, some people say that not everybody is called to be a missionary full time. But everybody is called to be involved in reaching the world. When you go one time, it absolutely changes your life. You get personally involved in this Great Commission. The Great Commission is not just for a few, but for all people who call themselves Christians.

Once you go and look in the eyes of the people who have never had a chance to hear the gospel and you realize you are the one bringing it to them, it absolutely changes you forever. It spoils you. It messes up your head because you realize that you have a purpose for living here in this world. You will never forget those eyes. Every time your church takes a missionary offering for the rest of your life, you will remember those eyes. You will remember the children. You will remember the older people. You will remember the people who gave their lives to the Lord and are going to heaven because you decided to go on a mission trip. You will remember that when you wrapped your arms around them, they hugged you back. You will remember giving them the love of God when all you did was give a week or a month of your life to bring them the gospel.

As a follower of Christ, you must realize that this is part of your life. This is how you are made. You cannot stay at home and forget those people are there. You cannot look at the globe and see it as just a ball with pieces of land on it.

People are all around the world. You take seriously God's commission to go. You take it personally. It is not that He is talking to everybody else. He is talking to you. It is as if Jesus is looking you right in the eyes and saying, "*You* go." Don't assume that somebody else is going to do it. *You* go. Even if you go only one time, you'll be changed for the good forever.

Continue to pray:

> *God, where do You want me to go? I am going to take Your commission seriously and personalize it and do something about it. I refuse to let everybody else do the work. I am going to personally do something about it sometime during my teen years. Lord, where could I go this summer? In Jesus' name, amen.*

Let Him begin to speak to your heart about it.

DAY 5

DON'T WORRY ABOUT THE MONEY

And my God shall supply all your need according to His riches in glory by Christ Jesus.

Philippians 4:19

Probably one of the biggest excuses I hear for not going to the mission field is that people don't think they can get enough money to cover the cost of the trip. Parents are afraid that their teenagers are going to beg money from them, and they don't think they have the money to send their teens. Teens are afraid that their parents will not give them any money and that no one else will either.

Reread today's verse and you'll realize there is no good excuse for not going on a mission trip. Money is an easy thing for God to get. He has tons of money. The Bible says He owns the cattle on a thousand hills (see Psalm 50:10). He will supply your needs. You simply have to go and find whose pockets He's keeping the money in. You may have to hold some fund-raisers and maybe some car washes. You will need to write some support letters. If you use all the energy you can muster, I guarantee you will get the money.

Getting the money is not the hard part. The hard part for God is getting you to say yes. It should be easy because this is such a fun deal. "You mean I get to go to another country? I get a chance to make history? I can help people who have never had a chance go to heaven and people are wanting to say no?" There is no good excuse to say no.

We at Global Expeditions have hundreds of testimonies from teenagers who have raised their money in a month or less. We have heard phenomenal stories about how God connected the money source and the need at exactly the right moment. If God has done that for other young people, He will surely do it for you. You have to understand that God definitely wants you to go. And if He wants you to go, then He will help you get the money.

When you apply to go on a Global Expeditions mission trip, we send you a whole package of information telling you everything you need to know to go on a mission trip, what to do and how to raise money. We have put together a booklet with about a million proven ideas to help you create momentum and excitement about your trip so that you can raise money for it. (Okay, that might be a bit of an exaggeration, but there are *a lot*.) These ideas are taken from other maniacs who have gone before and used these ideas to raise money. Don't you dare let money become a hindrance in your stepping out to do something to change the world.

I want you to copy Philippians 4:19 on an index card. Memorize it and meditate on it all day long. Chew on it until it becomes alive for you. Become convinced that God will supply your needs. I know He will, and I know there is a huge world to be reached. God knows that it will take money to go if you will say yes. Keep asking God where He wants you to go. Begin to do something active toward getting in the mission field. I don't care where you go, but *go!*

Think of ways you could start raising money for your mission trip. What things could your youth group do together to raise money?

What could you do on your own to raise money?

DAY 6

GOD STILL SENDS PEOPLE

For God so loved the world that He gave His only begotten Son, that whoever believes in Him should not perish but have everlasting life.

John 3:16

John 3:16 is a verse that, if you grew up in church, you have probably heard ever since you were a kid. But I want you to see something very clearly in it that you probably never thought about before. The Bible says that God "loved the world." It doesn't say that God loved *America* so much that He gave His only Son. The Bible doesn't say that God loved your town or your youth group so much that He gave His only Son. It doesn't even say that God just loved you so much that He gave His only Son. The Bible says that He loved *the world*.

When God decided to give His Son, He was looking at all the people all over the world for all time, and His heart was broken. He thought something like, *Whatever I have to do to win all the world back, I want to do it.* The fact is that 4.3 billion people still don't know that God sent His Son to save the world. They don't know that He loved the world so much that He gave His very best—His Son.

The Bible says that He gave *His only Son*. He didn't rain tracts down from the sky. He didn't send an email or a text message. He sent a person. He sent His own flesh and blood because He wanted the people of the world to know that His love was not something abstract. He wanted a human being to come down and show this world what His love was like. He didn't want to just tell people through some written message; He wanted to show them.

So when Jesus came and hugged the children, the arms of God were wrapped around their necks. When He came and gave back dignity to people who were depressed and messed up, they could look in His eyes and see His compassion. When He healed them and placed His hands on them and showed them the Father's love, they could understand and relate to it. They could understand that God loved them so much He sent a human being, His own Son, to show them what He Himself was like.

And just as God expressed His love to the world in the person He sent, He still sends people today. He sends people like you and me. He sends people full of the love of God, people who have had a life-changing encounter with God, people full of the fire of a God who gave His life for them. That's the kind of people He sends out to change the world. If you have made a commitment to be a follower of Christ, then you are that kind of person. I believe that you have had an encounter with God and that you will never be the same.

"For God so loved the world that He gave His only begotten Son." God gave His very best. Let me ask you something: Do you love God so much that you're willing to give Him your best, to give a summer of your life, to give a month or two months, to give your whole life if necessary? God gave His very best to get the job done—to save the people who believe in Him—and He is looking for Christ followers who will give their best to get the job done—to reach the entire world with the gospel.

There is no more time for talk. It is time to get out there and reach the world. As a follower of Christ, you need to stand up and be counted and do something about changing the world.

Pray this prayer:

God, where do You want me to go? I'm ready to go. I'm going to be one of those people who go just like You sent Your Son. I'm ready to go, too, Lord. Send me, and I will go. In Jesus' name, amen.

If you never have before, memorize John 3:16 right now. Meditate on it today, and really think about the depth of God's love for *all* of the world.

DAY 7

COMMIT TO GO!

But His word was in my heart like a burning fire shut up in my bones; I was weary of holding it back, and I could not.

Jeremiah 20:9

We've been talking throughout this book about changing the world, and you've been thinking about playing your part to change the world. You've been getting your heart stirred up about living for God and loving Him and serving Him every day. Now it's time to do something about it. It's time to make plans to go.

We Christians have been talking about changing the world, praying about changing the world, writing books about changing the world and having conferences about changing the world. But only a few have done much about actually reaching the world compared to the number of people who claim to be Christians. Most Christians have been doing everything except changing the world! Now is the time to slam on the brakes, stop everything in your life and say, "Lord, if I don't do anything else, I'm going to make my life count for changing the world. I'm going to do something about it right now."

Whatever plans you have for this upcoming summer, they're worth changing. God has a more important agenda. He wants to use you to change the world. Quit thinking that it's everybody else's responsibility. It's time to take personal responsibility. As a Christ follower, you are a different breed of Christian. You're someone set apart from the average, boring, lifeless, cheesy, lazy, low-life, couch-potato slug-of-a-Christian. You are somebody who is determined to do something that really matters with your life.

The very fact that you have made it to this point in this book shows that you are determined to go after God with all your heart. Now is the time to step out of your comfort zone and actually do something about it. You have been praying all along, *Lord, will You use me? God, do You want to use me?* Now it's time for you to hear His heart say, "Yes, I want to use you. Now go for it!"

Some people seem to be waiting for lightning from heaven to strike them or for an audible voice to say, "Go ye, therefore." Well, guess what?! He has already said to go. Now it's time for you to obey. He may speak to you in a still, small voice and put a strong desire in your heart. Good! Go for it. The Bible says that He gives you the desires of your heart—He puts the desire inside of you to do these things (see Proverbs 21:1).

Do you feel unspiritual because you just want to go for the adventure? That's okay. It's a valid reason to go, too. What a great adventure it is to do something that will change the world for God! To be honest with you, that's the first reason I went. I thought it would be fun to reach people for Jesus who had never had a chance to be reached before. As a result, I got a calling to be involved in missions for the rest of my life. God will take a misguided desire to have an adventure or to just do something good for Him and turn it into a life calling.

Make plans right now. Look at the application in the back of this book. Fill it out and mail it to us at Global Expeditions. We'll send you all the other information you need. We'll send you details on all the options for the different countries we are going to and how you can get there. You'll be amazed at what God will do through you as you do something about changing the world right now.

Don't be a follower of Christ in name only. Be a follower of Christ in deed. Join the thousands of young people who make a commitment to truly follow Christ and change the world.

God bless you as you make plans to go on a mission trip this summer, as you fill out your application and as you get ready to raise your money. God is so proud of you that you have made it all the way to the end of this book. You are just at the very beginning of a lifestyle of changing the world. Let your overseas world-changing experience begin this summer, and watch God use you literally to change the world. I look forward to seeing you this summer.

As a follower of Christ, I commit to go on at least one mission trip while I am still young. I will trust God for the money, and I'll go where He wants me to go. I commit to pray for the people of this world who do not know Jesus and have never had a chance to hear the gospel message.

______________________________ _______________

Your Signature Date

WEEK 13

BLASTING INTO THE REST OF YOUR LIFE

CELEBRATE! YOU MADE IT!

Those who are wise shall shine like the brightness of the firmament, and those who turn many to righteousness like the stars forever and ever.
Daniel 12:3

Congratulations! You made it! I know that your life has been changed as each day you have applied the things that have been suggested. Let's take some time and look back to see exactly what God has done in your life. It's important to do this so that you can really rejoice over what He has done.

What are two major things God has taught you these past 12 weeks?

What things have changed in your life?

What new habits do you have now?

How many Scripture verses have you memorized? ______________

What have you done to start changing the world?

____

____

____

____

____

____

How many people have you witnessed to? ______________

How many people were saved? (Remember, it is not your responsibility to get them saved; it is your responsibility to let them know about Jesus.) ______________

Wow! Don't you feel great?! Don't get a big head or anything, but you do have reason to celebrate what God has done to and through you. You shine like a star in the sky!

DAY 2

EVALUATING YOUR GROWTH

I press on, that I may lay hold of that for which Christ Jesus has also laid hold of me.

Philippians 3:12

Take a few minutes and read over what you wrote yesterday. Wow! Look at all the things that God has done in your life! Take some time right now and thank Him for what He has done through you.

As you grow in the Lord, every once in a while you need to look back to really appreciate all that God is doing in your life. Yes, you must "press on" like Paul explained in Philippians 3:12, but you also have to see how far you have come from time to time.

Think about what has happened in your heart in the past 12 weeks. What has God been stirring up inside you? How pure is your heart these days? With all the Scriptures you have memorized and all the time you have spent in prayer, how has your passion for Jesus increased?

____

____

____

____

____

Think about what has happened in your mind the past 12 weeks. What do you spend your time thinking about? When your mind drifts off, where does it go? (I am hoping that considering all you have learned, your mind now gets into the deep things of God.)

____

____

____

Think about what has happened to your strength in the past 12 weeks. How are you using it for God? How are you expressing your love for Him with your energy?

I am so proud of you, and I know that God is, too!

WHERE DO YOU GO FROM HERE?

I consider my life worth nothing to me, if only I may finish the race and complete the task the Lord Jesus had given me—the task of testifying to the gospel of God's grace.

Acts 20:24, *NIV*

Now it's time to focus on what to do with the rest of your life. You have just succeeded in a great accomplishment, but it is not the time to put on the brakes. Sometimes when you are at the top and you really succeed at something, you feel that you can back off a little, slow down, maybe even stop for a while. It is easy to think that you can live on "yesterday's manna."

But look at what happened when David did that. He had won all those wars. He had made the whole kingdom his. He had killed a bear and a lion and Goliath (see 1 Samuel 17). But he began to coast on his victories; and instead of going out and winning more battles, he let the army go out on their own to fight. (Kings never did that back then; they always led the troops.) That is when he saw Bathsheba, and he blew it big time! Read 2 Samuel 11 for the whole story.

So, you see, you can't quit fighting the fight of faith now! This is only the beginning! Followers don't back off; they go on to win other victories. Look at Hebrews 10:39: "We are not like those people who turn back and get destroyed. We will keep on having faith until we are saved" (*CEV*).

This book is more than a 13-week devotional; it is a call to commit to a whole new lifestyle. This is not a whim; it is serious Christianity. This is not just a good idea; this is the recipe for a great life with God!

What are your goals for this week?

What victories are you reaching for?

TRACKING YOUR COMMITMENTS

Continue to work out your salvation with fear and trembling, for it is God who works in you to will and to act according to his good purpose.

Philippians 2:12-13, *NIV*

The things that you have begun to do, you should continue for the rest of your life. Just go ahead and plan on doing that right now.

Look at the chart at the end of this book (appendix B), and starting next week, begin filling it in to show the progress you are making with all of your commitments.

So far this week, how have you been doing with each of your commitments (look at appendix B for a list of them)? Briefly evaluate your progress.

DAY 5

NO TURNING BACK

Be careful to do as the Lord your God had commanded you: you shall not turn aside to the right hand or to the left. You shall walk in all the ways which the Lord your God has commanded you.

Deuteronomy 5:32-33

Get your heart and mind set to go for it—at least through your teen years. Followers of Christ live an intense Christian lifestyle. All of their teen years, they keep the commitments we've talked about. You can do it. I know. I was fired up about Jesus in my teen years, and I never turned my back on Him. Sure, I've made mistakes along the way, but I've never walked away from God.

About two weeks after I gave my life to God, a man told me something that totally wrecked my plans. He said, "You can really only backslide one time in your life." I thought, *Yeah, right. I have big plans, buddy.*

He went on to explain: "When you first give your life to the Lord and then fall away accidentally, God can understand. But when you come back to the Lord, you then realize the mistake you made and you cannot do it 'accidentally' again. Now if you get away from God, you are not backsliding but intentionally turning your back on Him and walking away."

I thought, *Great! Now I don't have a choice. I have to stay on fire because I'm sure not going to intentionally turn my back on God!* So I didn't. I didn't think I had a choice. Going up and down—being on fire and falling away—was no longer an option. That man spoiled all of my plans.

Now I have just spoiled yours!

I never told you that keeping your commitments would be easy, but some commitments are probably easier for you to fulfill than others. Which commitments come pretty easily to you?

Which commitment(s) do you have to work harder on so that you don't backslide?

DAY 6

STANDING FIRM

He who stands firm to the end will be saved.

Matthew 24:13, *NIV*

The Bible talks about standing firm over and over. "All men will hate you because of me, but he who stands firm to the end will be saved" (Matthew 10:22, *NIV*). "If we endure, we shall also reign with Him. If we deny Him, He also will deny us" (2 Timothy 2:12).

Being a follower of Christ is about standing firm until the end. It's about enduring, no matter what the cost. It's not about barely making it to heaven but about blazing a trail there and taking a lot of other people with you! It's not hoping for it; it's actually doing it. And you are not prideful just because you are determined to live right and change the world. You are like Jesus.

If you really do the things we've talked about in this book—if you fulfill your commitments—you'll stand firm. I know because I do them, too.

Memorize today's Scripture verse right now. Meditate on it all day long and think about how you're going to stand firm until you achieve the reward of all the faithful: eternal life with Christ.

What sort of problems that might shake you up have you run into? What can you do when you feel as if someone or something is trying to shake you off your firm two feet?

DAY 7

COMMIT TO BE PART OF GOD'S ARMY

Like dawn spreading across the mountains a large and mighty army comes, such as never was of old nor ever will be in ages to come.

Joel 2:2, *NIV*

You have joined the Lord's army—an army of thousands of other teens in the U.S. and the rest of the world who are taking on the same challenge. They are tired of boring Christianity and are rising up to change the world. They are coming together as an army of young serious Christians who have decided to stand firm.

I can't make this decision for you. Your mom and dad can't decide for you. Your youth pastor can't decide for you. Even your accountability friends can't decide for you (although they can help you keep your commitment once you have made it). You have to decide on your own to stand firm.

Now is the time to stay focused on how you are going to live, at least through your teen years. Set your heart on your twentieth birthday. Get into your mind and heart right now the way you plan to live until then.

Make plans right now for what you will do between now and then to change the world. Think about talking about Jesus all the time and taking over your sports team one year and overtaking the places you hang out with your friends the next year. Think about the accountability friends you want to stick with all through your teen years. Think about going on a mission trip every summer until you turn 20. (Every summer? Yup. A lot of other teens have done it.) At least go one summer (*this year*)!

This is your chance to live free. Get into your Bible and stay there. Pick up the next Teen Mania devotional book. (Eventually there will be four of them, to take you through a whole year.) Live a life focused on Jesus, and go crazy to get others to do the same. Make your life count while you're young.

You are a cut above this world. God's hand is on your life. You can't back down now. There is too much at stake. Get other friends interested in becoming followers of Christ, too. You are what was prophesied about in Joel 2. You are the answer to millions of people's prayers for God to use the young people of the world.

All of history has been waiting for you to get to this point. Now all of heaven is watching to see what you will do to change the world with your life.

You must succeed; the world is counting on you. You have what it takes to make a big difference. You are a follower of Christ!

God, I commit to be a soldier in Your army. I want to be an invincible soldier for You. I commit to fight to change the world for You. I want to obey You and live my life for You. I am Yours to use. In Jesus' name, amen.

______________________________ _______________

Your Signature Date

APPENDIX A

RECORD OF SCRIPTURES MEMORIZED

Reference	Date	Verse

Reference	Date	Verse

Reference	Date	Verse

Reference Date Verse

Reference	Date	Verse

Reference	Date	Verse

Reference	Date	Verse

Reference Date Verse

Reference Date Verse

APPENDIX B

RECORD OF CONTINUING COMMITMENTS

Use this chart to track your commitments for weeks 14 through 31. List the number of days you had your quiet time, and then complete the information for the corresponding numbers below.

1. I have followed God's way of love and forgiveness this week. Ways I showed love and/or forgiveness this week.
2. I have been renewing my mind and changing the way I think this week. Weak areas I worked on this week.
3. I have been studying my Bible and meditating on God's Word this week. Scriptures I meditated on this week.
4. I have continued to surround myself with accountability friendships this week. Issues we have dealt with this week.
5. I have lived a lifestyle of holiness this week. Ways I worshiped or idols I cast down this week.
6. I have stayed pure this week. Situations in which I've stayed pure by my choices this week.
7. I have honored my parents in action and in attitude this week. Ways I've honored my parents this week.
8. I have attended my church and youth group this week. Ways I have shown my sense of belonging this week.
9. I have started a revolution in my world this week. Ways I have spread the gospel this week.
10. I have made preparations this week to go to the mission field. Preparations I have made this week.

Week 14 Date: ______________ Days I had quiet time: ______

1. ____________________
2. ____________________
3. ____________________
4. ____________________
5. ____________________
6. ____________________
7. ____________________
8. ____________________
9. ____________________
10. ____________________

Week 15 Date: ______________ Days I had quiet time: ______

1. ____________________
2. ____________________
3. ____________________
4. ____________________
5. ____________________
6. ____________________
7. ____________________
8. ____________________
9. ____________________
10. ____________________

Week 16 Date: ______________ Days I had quiet time: ______

1. ____________________
2. ____________________
3. ____________________
4. ____________________
5. ____________________
6. ____________________
7. ____________________
8. ____________________
9. ____________________
10. ____________________

Week 17 Date: ______________ Days I had quiet time: ______

1. ______________________________
2. ______________________________
3. ______________________________
4. ______________________________
5. ______________________________
6. ______________________________
7. ______________________________
8. ______________________________
9. ______________________________
10. ______________________________

Week 18 Date: ______________ Days I had quiet time: ______

1. ______________________________
2. ______________________________
3. ______________________________
4. ______________________________
5. ______________________________
6. ______________________________
7. ______________________________
8. ______________________________
9. ______________________________
10. ______________________________

Week 19 Date: ______________ Days I had quiet time: ______

1. ______________________________
2. ______________________________
3. ______________________________
4. ______________________________
5. ______________________________
6. ______________________________
7. ______________________________
8. ______________________________
9. ______________________________
10. ______________________________

Week 20 Date: ______________ Days I had quiet time: ______

1. ______________________________
2. ______________________________
3. ______________________________
4. ______________________________
5. ______________________________
6. ______________________________
7. ______________________________
8. ______________________________
9. ______________________________
10. ______________________________

Week 21 Date: ______________ Days I had quiet time: ______

1. ______________________________
2. ______________________________
3. ______________________________
4. ______________________________
5. ______________________________
6. ______________________________
7. ______________________________
8. ______________________________
9. ______________________________
10. ______________________________

Week 22 Date: ______________ Days I had quiet time: ______

1. ______________________________
2. ______________________________
3. ______________________________
4. ______________________________
5. ______________________________
6. ______________________________
7. ______________________________
8. ______________________________
9. ______________________________
10. ______________________________

Week 23 Date: ______________ Days I had quiet time: ______

1. ______________________________
2. ______________________________
3. ______________________________
4. ______________________________
5. ______________________________
6. ______________________________
7. ______________________________
8. ______________________________
9. ______________________________
10. ______________________________

Week 24 Date: ______________ Days I had quiet time: ______

1. ______________________________
2. ______________________________
3. ______________________________
4. ______________________________
5. ______________________________
6. ______________________________
7. ______________________________
8. ______________________________
9. ______________________________
10. ______________________________

Week 25 Date: ______________ Days I had quiet time: ______

1. ______________________________
2. ______________________________
3. ______________________________
4. ______________________________
5. ______________________________
6. ______________________________
7. ______________________________
8. ______________________________
9. ______________________________
10. ______________________________

Week 26 Date: ______________ Days I had quiet time: ______

1. ____________________
2. ____________________
3. ____________________
4. ____________________
5. ____________________
6. ____________________
7. ____________________
8. ____________________
9. ____________________
10. ____________________

Week 27 Date: ______________ Days I had quiet time: ______

1. ____________________
2. ____________________
3. ____________________
4. ____________________
5. ____________________
6. ____________________
7. ____________________
8. ____________________
9. ____________________
10. ____________________

Week 28 Date: ______________ Days I had quiet time: ______

1. ____________________
2. ____________________
3. ____________________
4. ____________________
5. ____________________
6. ____________________
7. ____________________
8. ____________________
9. ____________________
10. ____________________

Week 29 Date: ________________ Days I had quiet time: ______

1. ____________________
2. ____________________
3. ____________________
4. ____________________
5. ____________________
6. ____________________
7. ____________________
8. ____________________
9. ____________________
10. ____________________

Week 30 Date: ________________ Days I had quiet time: ______

1. ____________________
2. ____________________
3. ____________________
4. ____________________
5. ____________________
6. ____________________
7. ____________________
8. ____________________
9. ____________________
10. ____________________

Week 31 Date: ________________ Days I had quiet time: ______

1. ____________________
2. ____________________
3. ____________________
4. ____________________
5. ____________________
6. ____________________
7. ____________________
8. ____________________
9. ____________________
10. ____________________

TEEN MANIA'S MISSION STATEMENT:

To provoke a young generation to passionately pursue Jesus Christ and to take His life-giving message to the ends of the earth!

Acquire the Fire
BattleCry
Center for Creative Media
Global Expeditions
Honor Academy
Local Church Partnerships

www.teenmania.org